THE BEST DAMN COMMERCIAL REAL ESTATE INVESTING BOOK EVER WRITTEN!

*What I wish I knew
BEFORE becoming a
commercial real estate investor*

MONICA VILLASENOR

VILLASENOR
Productions

This publication is designed to provide competent and reliable information regarding the subject matter covered. However, it is sold with the understanding that the author and publisher are not engaged in rendering legal, financial, or other professional advice. Laws and practices often vary from state to state and are subject to change. If legal or other expert assistance is required, the services of a professional should be sought. The author and publisher specifically disclaim any liability that is incurred from the use or application of the contents of this book.

If you have purchased this book without a cover, you should be aware that this book may have been stolen property and reported as "unsold and destroyed" to the publisher. In such case neither the author nor the publisher has received any payment for this "stripped book."

All photographs used on the cover courtesy of Tim and Brynda Nelson, Nelson Photography
www.nelsonphotography.net

Visit the author's website www.monicavillasenor.net

Published by Villasenor Productions, LLC
All rights reserved.

Villasenor Productions, LLC
10300 W. Charleston Blvd. #13-360
Las Vegas, NV 89135
villasenorproductions@yahoo.com

Library of Congress Control Number: 2007903840

Printed in the United States of America

ISBN: 978-0-9793646-0-0

First Edition: March 2007

Dedication

This book wouldn't be possible without the support and sacrifice of many different people. Specifically I want to thank my awesome husband, Mike, who is, and continues to be the man of my dreams. Thank you to my children, Camden and Connor, who remind me daily to laugh. Life is fun! Thank you to my mom, Candy, who has never told me, "You can't do that." And, thank you to my sister April, whose passing has enabled me to realize at a young age how precious life is.

TABLE OF CONTENTS

INTRODUCTION

Real estate investing is hot right now! You see it in thousands of books that are written about real estate investing. You see it's popularity in infomercials about buying real estate for no money down and in such televison programs as *Flip This House* and *Property Ladder*. I'm sure I don't have to convince you of the benefits of real estate, as I would be preaching to the choir. But, what I will do, is show you how commercial real estate investments are far superior to residential real estate investments.

I KNOW EVERYTHING....NOT!!!

I want to let you know what I am, and what I am not. I am a full time real estate investor who for the last three years has been finding, analyzing, and closing on commercial real estate properties. I am NOT a guru. I don't have that "one special secret" that will make you a millionaire by investing in real estate. The fact is, there are only a certain number of ways to make money in real estate, which have been around for decades. These money making strategies are recycled and packaged differently, and then marketed as "secrets" to wealth through real estate.

When I began my journey into the commercial real estate investing world, I had no knowledge of how to do it. My first step was to try to find a book as a guide, to learn from other people's experiences, and hopefully, not mess up too badly. I went to the library. I went to the book store. I checked online. While I could find thousands of books on residential real estate investing, I just couldn't find many sources, maybe one or two books, about commercial real estate investing. I literally couldn't find one book that specifically addressed how to make the transition from residential real estate investing to commercial real estate investing.

PLAYING A DIFFERENT GAME

Maybe, it's all the same, I thought. But, I quickly found out that it's not. Commercial real estate investing is a whole different ball game from residential real estate investing. It's like comparing major league baseball to tee ball. It's the same game, but vastly different at the same time. I realized that the rules of the commercial real estate game were different than the rules of the residential real estate game. The problem was, I had no rule book to guide me along. I learned the rules of the game by playing it. Of course, I learned the most about the game by making mistakes. Not small mistakes either, but big ol' whopper mistakes. I am here to let you learn from my mistakes.

After a few years of commercial real estate investing experience under my belt, I was curious to see what new commercial real estate investing books had come out. I was interested to see if any of them contained information that could help me expand on what I had learned. Once again, I found a couple of commercial real estate investing books, but they were surprisingly bad. I say this because the authors wrote about things that I did not find important to know about, while leaving out information that I thought were crucial-such things as:

- The common mistakes novice commercial real estate investors make.

- How commercial real estate investing is different from residential real estate investing.

- How to analyze commercial real estate.

- What to expect during the process of purchasing commercial real estate.

- The author's real-life lessons learned from investing in commercial real estate.

The existing books written about commercial real estate investing lack critical items that a novice commercial real estate investor should know. I decided to be the person who would solve this problem by writing a "tell it like it is" book, which would serve as a guide for real estate investors on how to transition from residential real estate investing to commercial real estate investing.

NEW SUBJECTS ARE ALWAYS DIFFICULT TO LEARN AT FIRST

Do you remember when you were first learning how to drive a car? You had to think of every action. But, after you had been driving a while, you could arrive at a destination without even thinking about it, while talking on your cell phone with your kids screaming in the back seat. Anytime you start a new profession for the first time, it's tough. It's a struggle. You make mistakes. I certainly was no exception.

I wanted to write this book while I still considered myself a commercial real estate investing novice, before I got to the point where it was effortless and easy. I don't want to forget the details of the expensive lessons I learned. I wanted to make sure that the lessons learned were written down on paper, while they were fresh in my mind. I am not a commercial real estate investing "guru." I don't have experience in every single area of commercial real estate investing, but then again, nobody does. However, I do have enough experience at this point to give you a good start into the commercial real estate investment game.

WHAT TO EXPECT FROM THIS BOOK

This book is not written for beginning real estate investors. There are thousands of books available on investing in residential real estate for novice residential real estate investors. Get some experience in the residential investing world, then come back to this book. I am writing this book for those residential real estate investors who have some experience under their belt and are ready to take it to the next level. I will not be defining real estate terms that you should already know from investing in residential real estate, such as "loan to value." I will only define those terms unique to commercial real estate investing.

You will find that sometimes I go into great detail about one subject, while other times I breeze over other subjects. With the detailed subjects, you can assume that I've either had quite a bit of experience with the subject or it's an area I feel extremely passionate about. I will let you know if I haven't had any experience with a certain subject of commercial real estate investing as well. As you read through this book, you'll probably figure out that I'm quite opinionated and blunt about things.

That's just how I am.

The first few chapters of this book will mentally and emotionally prepare you for investing in commercial real estate. The more refined, in detail, aspects of commercial real estate investing will follow.

Each one of these chapters could be an entire book on it's own. I had no choice but to condense this book down to include only the most critical information that a novice commercial real estate investor should know about investing in commercial real estate. I will always share with you my personal experiences as a full time commercial real estate investor for the last three years, so you understand the basis of why I say what I do. This book is almost like my autobiography for the last three years. I hope you enjoy it. Happy reading!

CHAPTER 1
HOW IT ALL BEGAN

MY SOB STORY

It was like any other ordinary day at the dental office where I had worked as a dental hygienist for over five years. I loved the large office with the variety of dentists and coworkers. I also loved that I had developed long term relationships with my patients. I had just called in my last patient of the day. The patient sat in the chair, where I proceeded to put his patient napkin on. Just then, I was interrupted by the office manager. "I need to see you right now," she said. I excused myself from the patient. "I'll be right back." I told him, then turned to follow the manager into her office. "Monica, you are being terminated." she said bluntly, without any emotion.

Was this a sick joke? I thought. I was five months pregnant. I was the best hygienist they had. I had a die-hard patient following. I was the breadwinner in my family. And, at that moment, I was unemployed. I never saw it coming. I returned back to my room to start what would be my last patient at that office, but the office manager had already told the other dental hygienist that he would need to clean my last patient's teeth for me. My fellow dental hygienist knew I was being fired before I did. How humiliating!

I gathered my things and gave my coworkers a big hug. As I walked out the door for the last time, I wondered how many of them knew I was going to be fired before I had. I called my husband on my way home and told him what just happened. "Are you kidding?" he asked. "No," I said. I didn't buy for a minute the reason the office manager gave me for my termination (A confidentiality agreement forbids me from discussing it). I was shocked and embarrassed. I had never been fired before.

I was upset, but my husband was far more upset than I was. Confused at my apparent lack of rage, the only explanation I could give him was that I believe, "things happen for a reason." Another reason why I wasn't as devastated about being fired as I probably should have been, was because I had won a $30,000 jackpot playing bingo the week before. The timing of winning that bingo jackpot didn't seem coincidental to me.

"Life's challenges are not supposed to paralyze you. They're supposed to help you discover who you are."
Bernice Johnson Reagon

The first few days that I would normally have been at work were odd for me. I felt lost. At that point, my whole identity was as a dental hygienist. What do I tell people I do when they ask? What do I say when I am asked why I don't work at that dental office anymore? I should have just taken the time off to relax. But I couldn't. Relaxing is just not in my genetic make-up. I am the type of person who always has to be doing something.

Sometimes, when drastic, unforeseen events happen in your life, it forces you to reflect on which direction you want your life to go. I am the type of person who needs to feel like I'm constantly growing and learning. When I reach one goal, there's always another one, even bigger to replace it. For me, most of the fun in doing something new, is just seeing if I can do it.

I had gotten complacent in my life. When you have a good paying job, it's so easy to do. You get up, go to work, go home. The next day you get up, go to work, then go home. The following day, repeat again. You get your two weeks of vacation each year. That's the good life. Isn't it?

Sometimes when drastic, unforeseen events happen in your life, it forces you to reflect on which direction you want your life to go.

I did have the good life, but something was missing. I had accomplished the difficult process of becoming a dental hygienist, but I hadn't taken on a new challenge since then. I had been going through the motions of my life, instead of making the life I was meant to have. I had suppressed my need for personal growth because I had a beautiful house to pay for and a child, with another on the way. I just didn't feel I was in the financial position to risk everything to pursue the unknown.

Being fired was the kick in my butt I needed. It's like someone was telling me, "Hey, if you won't do it voluntarily, I'll do it for you."

9

Chapter One

What really intrigued me was real estate. Before I was fired, I had started investing in residential real estate and was quite successful at it. My husband and I sold a purchase option we had on a parcel of land for a $45,000 profit. We had also put some money down on a house we planned to "flip" when it was finished being built. When we purchased the home we live in now, we opted to rent our condo we had just moved from. We purchased our home just in the nick of time, as the crazy Las Vegas real estate market caused our $413,000 house to appreciate to $700,000 in less than two years.

I had also read *Rich Dad, Poor Dad,* by Robert Kiyosaki. That book made total and complete sense to me. It forever changed the way I would think about money, being an employee, and the importance of taking control over my own financial future.

I was at a fork in the road. Should I sit back until I delivered my son and then return to the dental hygiene profession? Or, should I take the chance to pursue real estate investing on a full time basis?

Being fired just reinforced to me what Robert Kiyosaki had written. As an employee, you are disposable. It doesn't matter what the reason is, if there even is one. As an employee, your financial future is at the whim of someone else. I decided that I would never allow anyone to control my financial future again. If I wanted to be in control, I couldn't return to dental hygiene. The decision was made. Full time real estate investor it was!

NOW WHAT?

I didn't want to focus on investing in residential real estate anymore. I needed to purchase real estate that generated enough positive cash flow to replace the income I had lost. As a dental hygienist, I usually took home about $4,400/month, after taxes. I needed to bring in at least the same amount of money.

It would take quite a while to purchase enough residential real estate to net $4,400. I didn't have a lot of time. I needed to replace the income I lost right away. Also, staying true to my need to grow, I felt I had acquired enough knowledge about real estate investing at that point to step up to commercial properties. They had to be the same, just bigger. Right? I couldn't have been more wrong.

WHAT NOBODY TELLS YOU

1. Commercial real state investing is a whole different ball game than residential real estate investing.
2. There really are no "secrets" to making millions of dollars in real estate. There is only information you haven't learned yet.
3. Mistakes are great learning experiences.
4. Your job is never secure.
5. Being fired can be great!
6. Question whether you are just going through the motions of your life or if you are creating the life you were meant to have.

CHAPTER 2
DO YOU HAVE THE GUTS?

Some professions, such as a fire fighter or a construction worker, require great physical strength. If you plan on succeeding in commercial real estate investing, you must have a different kind of strength. You must have mental strength. Commercial real estate investing is extremely mentally challenging. Frankly, not a lot of people have the stomach for it. It has been a great challenge for me and I'm the most stubborn person I know. The old saying, "If it was easy, everyone would be doing it." rings true with commercial real estate investing.

If you are the type of person who gives up easily when the going gets tough, I suggest you put this book down. It simply won't do you any good. While having knowledge is essential, that in itself, is not enough. There must also be action. What

> "Opportunities are usually disguised as hard work, so most people don't recognize them."
> Ann Landers

good does it do you to have a bunch of knowledge in your head, if you won't do anything with it? However, if you are the type of person who understands that with great trials, comes great rewards, then this book will prove helpful.

The first commercial real estate transaction you do will be tough. You won't know what you are doing. When you feel overwhelmed, please remember these things:

● Every single person who is an absolute real estate investing genius, once knew as much as you do right now.

● Nobody knows everything, nor ever will.

● You are just as smart and capable of becoming a commercial real estate investor as anyone else.

So, are you ready to join the real estate big leagues? Are you ready to play with the big boys (and girls)? Almost everyone is capable, but few people have the guts.

WHAT ARE YOU AFRAID OF?

It is normal to go into a situation you've never been in before with a bit of fear. My husband, Mike, is the king of the, "what if's." For example, Mike and I had been living in a condo with a $1,000/month mortgage payment. We decided it was time to move into a house, as our condo was too small for a family. The home we wanted to purchase would have a $2,400/month mortgage payment. Increasing our monthly mortgage payment that much was unfathomable to Mike. He repeatedly asked me, "Are you sure we can afford this?"

When we received final loan approval to purchase our home, we had to find a renter for the condo. "What if we can't find a good tenant? What if they destroy everything? Who is going to manage the property?" Mike asked me with concern. Mike had to be constantly assured that everything would work out fine. Every single property we have purchased since that time, he has expressed the same fears. With each real estate investment we do, he gets a bit more comfortable. However, even still to this day, he voices his fears all the time about the "what if's."

There will always be things that COULD go wrong. Most of the time, they won't. With each commercial property you look at, with every purchase offer you write, with every property inspection you perform, and with every property you purchase, your fears will slowly dissipate.

LISTEN TO OTHERS, BUT TRUST YOURSELF

Everyone Has Their Two Cents

Picture this scenario. You bring your car into the shop to have it's oil changed. You're making small talk with the mechanic about how you need to do some yard work. Your mechanic chimes right in and tells you, "You shouldn't water your grass for more than four minutes at a time, and don't cut the grass on the lowest setting, or it will get burnt." Should you blindly accept what he says as truth? Absolutely not! If you have questions about landscaping, you should ask someone who makes the majority of their income from that profession-a landscaper.

Chapter Two

It seems that everyone has an opinion about investing in real estate. They may have had a good experience, a bad experience, or no experience at all. Have you ever noticed that the majority of negative feedback and opinions come from people who are in a worse financial position than you? You must take a look at who is giving the opinion. Are they an expert in the field in which they speak? Do they make the majority of their income doing what it is they are advising you to do? If they are so financially savvy, why do they need a job?

Everyday people are bombarded by unsolicited advice from people who tell them why something won't work, when they have no expertise in the area in which they speak. What's worse, most people listen to the ill advice!

**"I owe my success to having listened respectfully to the best advice and then going away and doing the exact opposite."
G.K Chesterton**

Sometimes Even "Experts" Are Wrong

There may even be times when you seek advice from people who are experts in their respective field, but your gut tells you they're wrong. Columbus was told by many "experts" that the world was flat. His gut told him otherwise. Trust yourself!

I have faced this situation more than once. The most notable circumstance was when Mike and I decided to purchase a house to "flip." It was during the time the real estate market was going crazy here in Las Vegas. I knew it would take a minimum of six months for the house to be built, and with each month, the prices were increasing $10,000-$15,000. We wanted to catch this crazy wave of appreciation.

There were waiting lists of over 500 people at each builder's development. You would put your name on their list. Then, every couple of weeks, the builder would release nine, or so, homes in a phase. Prospective purchasers would need to show up at the builder's sales office, where they would literally pull names out of a hat for those people who were on the list and physically present that day. Those lucky people would enter into a purchase contract.

The particular builder of the home we wanted to purchase allowed only one investor per phase. This was critical because not only would we need our name pulled, we would need our name pulled before another investor's name was pulled.

We showed up on the designated day and were lucky enough to have our name picked. Because we were investors, we had to put $9,000 down as an earnest deposit ($1,500 for non investors). We didn't have the full $9,000, so we brought a credit card check and signed away. We were ecstatic!

The next day, we called our real estate agent, George (not his real name), to tell him the good news. He was happy, until he found out which lot we chose. Our particular lot was facing a new high school. He felt that trying to resell a home facing straight across from the high school would be a problem. He thought we should wait until the next phase to get a "better" lot location within the development.

> **Columbus was told by many "experts" that the world was flat.**

I disagreed. It was a brand new high school in a good area. If anything, I felt it would help the resell value. I also felt that waiting to purchase the home until the next phase was too risky. First, it was unknown if our name would be pulled again. Second, even if we were lucky enough to have our name pulled again, the purchase price would have increased $10,000-$15,000. I really appreciated George's concern, as we had a long history of friendship, but my gut told me I was right.

When I called George to tell him we were going to proceed with the purchase anyway, he once again warned me against it. I was starting to get mad. I knew I was right, but for some reason, he wouldn't let up. When I wouldn't listen to his advice, he thought he might have better luck getting through to my husband.

Mike called me. "Isn't he the Realtor? Doesn't he know what a good investment is? Maybe we should listen to him." he said, voicing his concern. "No," I replied. "George's job is to show us the properties. It's not his job to decide which property we should buy. He is totally crossing the line."

Going against George's advice, we proceeded with the purchase. The property took a year to be built. With each month that passed, the property continually appreciated. Once completed, we literally sold the property two days after we bought it, netting a $75,000 profit. I used that profit as part of the down payment for the purchase of my first commercial property, a 57 unit apartment complex in Windham, Ohio.

It seems that my gut was right after all. If I had listened to George, and not trusted myself, it could have been a very costly mistake.

IGNORE THE NO'S

My four year old son, Camden, is the best negotiator in the world. I swear, I'm going to hire him to negotiate my real estate deals when he gets older. It never fails. If he knows that every day he gets two vitamins, he'll ask for four. If I say he can have one sip of soda, he'll say, "Okay, three sips." No matter what I say, he'll always make a counter offer! On one hand, I LOVE IT! But as his mom, it drives me nuts!

I always try to be careful about how I word things with my children. On one hand, I love that Camden asks me over and over for something, even though I've already told him "no." It's a quality that those of us who are parents, try to nix out of our kids. It provides quite an interesting situation then, as to how to let your kids know that the answer truly is "no," without telling them to stop asking. I never want my kids to stop asking.

When we were growing up, our parents told us over and over again to "stop asking." Then, as adults, when we are told "no," we drop the subject. We accept the answer because we were brought up to believe that once we get a "no," it's over. You have to go back to being a kid in this sense. Keep asking. "No" doesn't mean "no," most of the time. It simply means that there isn't enough information provided to get to a "yes" yet.

The most notable time when I was able to convert a "no" to a "yes" was when I decided to convert an apartment complex in Redding, California to condominiums.

The City of Redding had never had a condo conversion

19

application before, nor had I ever done a condo conversion. One of the city's condo conversion codes mandated that the property had to be on a minimum of three acres. My property was on only 1.30 acres. I submitted the preapplication so we could address that specific issue.

The city sent the preapplication back to me with a letter that read, "Ms. Villasenor, your property does not qualify for a condominium conversion, as it does not meet the minimum three acre requirement." Ya think? That was the whole point of submitting the preapplication! Additionally, I sent the mayor an email with what I had in mind. He replied back and basically said, "I don't see the benefit." I didn't get any support there either.

If I was like most people, my condo conversion project would have been over before it had begun. But I'm not like most people. What the city didn't realize at the time, was that I had already made up my mind that the condo conversion was going to happen. Once the city understood that I was serious and would not just go away, they were quite pleasant to work with. With a lot of persistence and communication with the city, the condo conversion was eventually approved. It wasn't easy, but I made it happen!

> What the city didn't realize at the time, was that I had already made up my mind that the condo conversion was going to happen.

Another example of ignoring a "no" involves my parents. My dad's disability income was going to be ending, cutting his income in half. For my parents, losing that income would be financially devastating.

I suggested to my dad that a solution for his financial situation could be a reverse mortgage. My parents had owned their home forever. The property had a small mortgage balance of $50,000 on it. My dad was initially hesitant to apply for a reverse mortgage because he didn't want to increase the property's mortgage balance. He wanted to be able to pass on the greatest amount of money to his children as possible. I helped him realize that he needed to take care of his financial situation first. His children don't want to see him stressed out about how he's going to financially survive with half of his income gone. My dad also finally realized that his house will continue to appreciate, which will offset the increase to the property's loan balance that results from a reverse mortgage.

After attending a reverse mortgage seminar, my dad told me that everything sounded great, but he was told he couldn't do it because my mom was under 62 years old. He had stopped thinking it was a possibility because he was told "no." I knew better.

I advised him to call the lender to ask if he could put the property into a trust, for estate planning purposes, after the loan closed. The lender confirmed that it was acceptable. That was exactly what was needed to make the situation work. He removed my mom from the property's title, then completed the reverse mortgage paperwork. After the loan funded, he transferred the title of the property into a trust, then added my mom as a beneficiary. Not only did this situation meet the lender's requirements, but it was also a smart asset planning move.

Instead of paying a $500 monthly mortgage payment to the lender, my dad now makes no mortgage payment. Right there he is $500/month ahead. Additionally, he receives a $500 check monthly from the lender. Combining the $500 monthly savings, with the monthly $500 check he receives from the lender, my dad is $1,000 ahead, each month.

There's always another way of doing something. Get creative. Ask questions. Do whatever it takes. If you really want something, NEVER accept "no" for an answer.

THINK OUTSIDE THE BOX

I want you to imagine the word "standard" written on a piece of paper. Play along with me now. Did you write it? Good. Now, put down your pen or pencil. Pick up the piece of paper with the word "standard" written on it. Crumble it into a ball and throw it in the trash. Are you getting my point yet?

There's usually a standard way of doing almost anything. Does it matter? Not really. Standard is boring. Standard is slow. Standard is old school. You will find many examples in this book how I was able to overcome obstacles by being creative and thinking outside the box.

The best example I have of this, is again, with the condo conversion in Redding, California. As I mentioned before, I initially did not receive the most overwhelming support from the city officials. I had not only my financial future on the line, but the financial future of my family and friends, who were my money investors. They were counting on me to get the project approved. I couldn't afford to just cross my fingers and hope that the seven planning commissioners would approve the project. I needed to come up with a plan to ensure it. I started by asking myself the following question,

"How can I get the planning commission to have a vested interest in seeing this project approved?"

There is an overwhelming need for affordable home ownership opportunities in California. If the planning commissioners said "no" to an affordable development, the public would frown upon that decision. The problem is, the general public doesn't pay much attention to what's going on with the local government. I had to make sure that the planning commissioners would have the pressure of knowing that if they denied my condo conversion application, it would get broadcast out to the world. That is why I created my reality show "The Making of a Millionaire." It was a strategy. In addition to having the added pressure of cameras at the planning commission meeting, I would also be able to utilize the television program as part of my marketing plan, when it came time to sell the condo units down the road.

There is a time to let things happen and a time to make things happen.

We never needed the added pressure of having the cameras at the planning commission meeting. The project would have probably been approved without them. However, the cameras did have an impact. The planning commissioners, who have the gift of gab, didn't ask us nearly as many questions as they did of all the other applicants. Kent, the city planner assigned to my project said, "I've never seen them so quiet." Then he looked over at me and said, "You just may be smarter than you're letting on." I was giggling inside. You betcha!

"The Making of a Millionaire," which started as a strategy, has grown into this whole other business. Not only will we generate revenue from the reality show itself, but there will be multiple streams of income created from merchandise sales, an electronic book, and stock footage licensing fees. Long term, we will probably make more money from my "strategy," than from the project itself. Now, that's being creative!

What would you have done? Would you have sat back hoping the planning commission would vote "yes?" How would you have handled the situation? I'm sure you could come up with some creative solutions that would have worked just as well as the television show idea.

Thinking creatively takes some practice, but once you start, your brain will come up with some wild ideas. You will be able to acquire a greater amount of commercial real estate if you are creative in writing up purchase contracts, obtaining financing, and coming up with ideas to improve your property's profit. By being creative, you can take an "okay" deal and make it great.

THINK BIGGER!

This saying was made famous by Donald Trump. But let's twist it a bit. Think bigger as far as the number of people you serve. I once read that the more people you serve as part of your business, the wealthier you will become. When you own residential real estate, you are serving one family. You are providing a nice, safe home for one family to live in. When you own commercial real estate, such as a retail building, you are serving the many people who come to that business everyday. You should always ask yourself the following question:

"How can I serve more people with this property?" The answer may surprise you.

Let's look at the example of my reality show again. Initially, the condo conversion project was only going to serve the 24 families that bought the condo units and the surrounding neighborhood from all of the improvements we were applying to the property.

When the television show is broadcast, millions of viewers will potentially benefit from the dramatic, entertaining, and inspirational program. Consequently, when only 24 families were benefitting from the project, the profit potential was great. But now, with the TV series, the profit potential is through the roof. The more people who view the TV series, the more money I make. See how that works? **I really am oversimplifying this concept because you never know what profound effect your positive actions have on someone's life.** Challenge yourself to find ways to serve more people. It doesn't always require more work.

Even I, sometimes, have to challenge myself to think big enough. For instance, with a condominium conversion project, it literally takes the same amount of time to convert 24 apartment units as it takes to convert 200 apartment units. It takes the same effort to get a loan for 24 units as it takes for 200 units. It takes the same effort to market 24 units as it takes to market 200 units. It takes the same time and effort to make a little money or a lot.

WHAT NOBODY TELLS YOU

1. Successful commercial real estate investing requires

focused mental strength.

2. Follow your gut. It never lies.

3. Even "professionals" and "experts" are wrong sometimes.

4. You should be more like your children.

5. A "no" is not a "no."

6. Being creative can be more fun than doing things the "standard" way.

7. The bigger you think, the richer you will become.

Chapter 3
Playing With The Big Boys
(And Girls)

S o, you are still reading. Congratulations! That means you must have the mental fortitude needed for this business. You are ready to take your real estate investing up a notch to start building an incredible portfolio of commercial real estate.

WHAT IS COMMERCIAL REAL ESTATE?

Just as there are many different types of residential real estate, such as single family homes, condominiums, town homes, and duplexes, there are also many different types of commercial real estate. Commercial real estate includes, but is not limited to, apartment buildings, retail buildings, industrial parks, mobile home parks, gas stations, strip malls, office buildings, hotels, and more. I need to clarify this further.

Apartment buildings containing five or more units, although residential in nature, are considered commercial real estate.

Chapter Three

Apartment buildings with one to four units are considered residential real estate. Commercial real estate, simply put, is anything that is not residential real estate or land.

However, commercial real estate investing isn't only limited to real estate itself. Investing in commercial real estate could be purchasing air, water, or mineral rights, which we will discuss later in the book.

WHY INVEST IN COMMERCIAL REAL ESTATE?

It's Easier To Get Financing

When qualifying for a loan to purchase residential real estate, the bank is looking at YOU-your credit score, your income, and your debts. Let's say that you are interested in purchasing a residential investment property for $100,000, that will rent for $1,000/month. In qualifying you for this loan, the bank will credit only 75% of the property's projected rental income, in this case $750, to offset the added mortgage expense from the property you are seeking to purchase. For banking purposes, each time you purchase a new residential investment property your financial statement will show that you are losing an additional $250 a month, when in reality you are not.

Each time you go to purchase another residential investment property, it will become increasingly difficult to qualify for financing, because your financial statement will show your cash flow becoming more and more negative. With as few as five residential investment properties, you would show a paper loss of $1,250/month. There will come a point when you will be able to qualify for a mortgage to purchase residential investment property, but only with terms that would kill the deal. When you reach that point, your only other alternatives would be to find properties where seller financing is offered or you would have to pay cash. That would limit the number of potential properties to choose from, which is not an ideal situation.

Qualifying for a commercial real estate loan doesn't work the same way as qualifying for a residential real estate loan. Commercial real estate lenders look at the property's income to qualify the loan. You, as the borrower, are a much smaller factor in the loan approval equation. If the property's cash flow doesn't meet certain criteria, (We'll discuss this more in Chapter 10) the lender won't approve the loan, even if you have the most beautiful credit in the world. On the opposite side of the spectrum, if your credit score is less than ideal, it may actually be easier to purchase commercial real estate, than it is to purchase residential real estate. I can hear all of the people with less than stellar credit rejoicing around the world!

There's Never Been A Better Time

The internet has leveled the commercial real estate investing playing field. Before the internet was around, there wasn't a centralized place to access commercial properties for sale. You would pretty much be limited to investing in commercial real estate located within your own state. If you happened to live in an expensive area, such as California, trying to find commercial properties to step up to would prove difficult.

That doesn't matter now. With access to the internet, you are not limited to investing in commercial properties located only in your local area and that's good news for you! It's also good news from a seller's perspective as well, as the entire world has access to their property listing, which translates into more potential buyers. With internet resources available to commercial real estate investors, such as you and I, the number of commercial properties for sale that you have access to is limited only by how quickly you can analyze each property.

More Commercial Real Estate is Needed

The United States just welcomed it's 300 millionth resident. The population is estimated to reach 400 million by the year 2042. As medical technology continues to increase the average life span, our population continues to increase. In addition to that, immigration to the United States continues to increase at a staggering rate. As the population increases, there will be a greater need for commercial real estate. Apartment buildings will be needed to provide housing. Long term care facilities will be in demand to provide an appropriate place to take care of the elderly. Mixed use developments with retail on the bottom and residential dwellings above, will be needed to provide a work/live solution.

There will also be a greater need for businesses to serve the expanded population. Those businesses will need to lease buildings to provide their products and services to their clients. With the law of supply and demand in force, the price of commercial real estate will continue to rise.

Inflation Happens

Just in the last two years, the cost of construction materials has doubled. America is competing on a global scale for materials and labor. In fact, I just read in the Las Vegas Review Journal, that China has bought half of the world's steel and glass supply. I also read that copper is in such demand, it's being stolen out of light poles and being sold for up to four dollar per pound. Why is this important?

It's to emphasize the fact that the cost of construction is going up at record levels. In addition to that, developmental fees, impact fees, and application fees must be paid to the city for the privilege of developing land. Those fees are consistently on the rise as well. On top of those two increases, the labor costs to build new buildings continues to increase. It's just a fact, that development, labor, and building costs are not going to decrease.

> **Do you really think that real estate prices, with the continual cost increase for labor, materials, land, and development fees will be cheaper ten years in the future, than it is today? If you think so, you may need a reality check.**

Think about the price of real estate ten years ago. Would you like to be purchasing real estate at the price it was then or at the price it is now? What about ten years in the future? Do you really think that real estate prices, with the continual cost increase for labor, materials, land, and development fees will be cheaper ten years in the future, than it is today? If you think so, you may need a reality check. Also realize that a dollar's buying power today, is greater than it's buying power in the future.

31

Chapter Three

Couple the rising costs of construction and development, with the continued increase in demand, and we have the making of a very nice situation for somebody's pocketbook. Hopefully, that somebody will be you. Make the increase of these costs an advantage to you, by purchasing commercial real estate at today's value, when you can lock in the price and a low interest rate.

The Power Of Leverage

For the past 36 years, real estate has been appreciating at an average rate of 6.34% per year. In fact, in that same period of time, there has never been a NATIONAL decrease in median prices of real estate (localized areas, such as California, have experienced temporary periods of decrease).

Couple the rising costs of construction and development, with the continued increase in demand, and we have the making of a very nice situation for somebody's pocketbook. Hopefully, that somebody will be you.

Many people compare this 6.34% rate of return for real estate investments with the typical 10% rate of return for stock market investments, as proof that investing in the stock market provides a superior rate of return. However, the rate of return is not comparing apples to apples. What the figure does not factor into the equation, is the fact that most people do not pay cash for real estate. Most people put some money down and obtain a mortgage for the remaining balance. The 6.34% appreciation rate, assumes that everyone paid cash for their property. It is not the true rate of return on the money that each one of us personally invests into a property.

Here's an example of two people who bought the exact same house and received the exact same appreciation rate of 6.34%. We'll see how the rate of return changes when utilizing the power of leverage, by obtaining a 90% mortgage.

Cash Buyer	**90% LTV Mortgage Buyer**
Purchase Price $200,000	Purchase Price $200,000
Cash Paid $200,000	Cash Paid $20,000
Appreciation $12,680	Appreciation $12,680
Return on money	Return on money
invested = **6.34%**	invested = **63.40%**

You can see that the buyer who utilizes the power of leverage with a 90% LTV mortgage, actually earns 57.06% more on their investment, than the person who does not use the power of leverage. The high investment return on real estate, accomplished by utilizing the power of leverage, makes the 10% rate of return you may get by investing in the stock market look down right pathetic. An additional factor to consider is that the rate of return comparison doesn't take into account the tremendous tax savings that real estate investments offer, which would push the real estate investment rate of return even higher.

Despite those facts, answer me this; Would you like a 6.34% rate of return on a $200,000 property or on a $2,000,000 property? Hmm...Should I take a $12,680 increase in my net worth or should I take a $126,800 increase in my net worth?

Chapter Three

Let me think about it. Okay, done. I'll take the $126,800 increase to my net worth. That difference, is the power of leverage. Not only do you get the benefit of appreciation on the money you personally put into the deal, but you *also* get the appreciation on the money that the bank puts into the deal, in the form of a mortgage.

It's The Quickest Route To Wealth

Given the choice between investing in residential real estate and investing in commercial real estate-which one would you choose? Which one provides the quickest path to wealth? The answer is commercial real estate. When you purchase commercial real estate, you are multiplying the power of leverage because the numbers are larger. Given the choice between investing in residential real estate or investing in commercial real estate, which one allows you to rapidly increase your equity, opening the door for further leveraging opportunities? Again, the answer is commercial real estate. Think bigger here. It's just another zero at the end, but what a difference it makes.

Less Competition

You see a ton of people who are jumping on the real estate investing band wagon. We've all seen the infomercials about how to flip houses, buy foreclosures, or purchase real estate with no money down. But 99% of those people are focusing on investing in residential real estate. I've yet to see an infomercial regarding any aspect of investing in commercial real estate.

Of those real estate investors who do move up from residential real estate investing to commercial real estate investing, they will generally purchase properties priced up to $1,000,000. Large corporations and Real Estate Investment Trusts (REIT) generally purchase commercial real estate starting at a price of $10,000,000. So, here we have this great potential of finding exceptional positive cash flowing commercial real estate for sale in the $1,000,000 to $10,000,000 price range, with limited competition.

There aren't many individual real estate investors who have the financial ability or the creativity, to come up with the typical 20-30% down payment needed to purchase commercial real estate. This lack of competition is a distinct advantage that commercial real estate investors have over residential real estate investors. However, you still must move quickly if you find a great deal.

Tax Savings

I'm sure you already realize the huge tax savings that comes from owning residential investment properties. So, just imagine what kind of tax savings you could have by owning commercial real estate. Commercial real estate takes the tax benefits of residential real estate and multiplies it. Not only do you make money, but with the current tax laws, you usually end up paying very little or no taxes at all.

It's actually quite bizarre to see on paper. As you buy more and more commercial real estate, your tax return will show you earning less and less, even though you actually made a profit.

It's actually quite bizarre to see on paper. As you buy more and more commercial real estate, your tax return will show you earning less and less, even though you actually made a profit. There's no other investment like it. With a loss from investing in stocks, there is no paper loss. You really did lose that money. On top of that, with a loss from investing in the stock market you can only write off a loss of $3,000/year on your taxes. If you lost $50,000 in the stock market, it would take you over 16 years to be able to write off the entire loss. With real estate investments, you can write off a loss of up to $25,000/year against your other income. If you are a "real estate professional," you can exceed that $25,000 loss.

I'm by no means an accountant. However, I can say, beyond a shadow of a doubt, that if you are paying income taxes, you don't own enough real estate.

INVESTING VERSUS SPECULATION

I've never heard anyone say, "I'm a real estate speculator." I've always heard people say, "I'm a real estate investor." The fact is, most of the people who say they are real estate investors, are not. They are speculators. If you purchase a property that generates a negative cash flow, betting instead on the property's appreciation, that is....

1. Speculation, and
2. Ummm, how shall I say this nicely? Stupid!!

I'll never understand why some people think it's okay to purchase real estate that generates a negative cash flow. Why? Why would you do that when you can easily find a property that generates a positive cash flow *and* appreciates at the same time? I'll never get it.

What you are really doing, when you purchase real estate for appreciation, and not for positive cash flow, is gambling. You might as well go to Las Vegas and put your money on black at the roulette table. There are literally thousands of properties that will appreciate just as well, and make you money in the mean time.

It's not investing if you buy a property, cross your fingers, and hope it appreciates. It IS investing when you buy a property for it's immediate positive cash flow. If the property appreciates, that's just icing on the cake. Investing is active with an immediate positive cash flow that is spendable.

IF YOU MUST SPECULATE

If only you could know where the next big development was going to happen. You would be able to buy a commercial property, wait for the development to catch up, get some nice appreciation, sell it, then take your fat check to the bank. If only...Hey, wait a minute. There is a way!

Most decent sized cities have televised city planning and city council meetings. It is a really good idea to see how this part of the government works. If you have to go through the subdivision or rezoning process, you should do this anyway. to prepare yourself for what to expect. Watching these meetings gives you information that could have a significant impact on the future appreciation of certain areas. Where's the next big freeway going to be? Where's the next major mall going? Where are the water and sewer lines expanding? A property without access to public utilities makes commercial development unlikely. When public utilities are brought to a property, as part of the city's long term growth plan, it makes the property much more valuable.

Most of the time, the local newspaper company will send a reporter to attend each meeting as well, so that they can report the most important developments to the general public. You see, this information is all public record. It's available for anybody who wants to view or access it. You can literally go into the city's planning department and ask to see the entire file for any particular development you please. Most of the time you won't need to know all of the details of a particular development, but if something is of particular interest, you can.

Most people don't watch these city meetings. I am the only one I know of, who will actually sit down and watch this kind of stuff. That is where your opportunity lies. By watching these government meetings, you will know months in advance, before 99% of the general population does, what developments are in the works and where they will be. You will have this information before a building permit is ever pulled. How much does having this information earlier than everyone else benefit you? Tremendously!

> You see, this information is all public record. It's available for anybody who wants to view or access it.

You want to find a property for sale surrounding a proposed development and buy it before the general public is aware that the development is coming. Let's say that a Lowe's is going to be built next year. Look for opportunities to invest in commercial real estate surrounding the proposed Lowe's site because the improvements and the increased traffic count, that comes as a result of this type of development, will make the surrounding commercial real estate more valuable.

If the city meetings are not televised, check to see if the city has a web site. If so, check under the developmental department page for the city's meeting agenda. If there is no website, then move. Just kidding! In that case, you may be stuck making a trip to city hall every two weeks to get the information. If you insist on speculating instead of investing, this is the way to do it.

MY SUGGESTED WEALTH STRATEGY

Start With What You Know

The first type of commercial real estate I would recommend for you to purchase is an apartment building (five or more units). You will learn a lot from your first commercial real estate transaction. You will make mistakes. It is better that you minimize those mistakes on your first deal, by purchasing a commercial property that is somewhat familiar to you. You already have the experience of looking for an investment property, writing up a purchase contract, performing an inspection, obtaining financing, closing the deal, finding tenants, and performing property management

> You will make mistakes. It is better that you minimize those mistakes on your first deal, by purchasing a commercial property that is somewhat familiar to you.

duties.

You should be looking to purchase a commercial property that generates a positive cash flow. Over time, you want to continue acquiring commercial real estate that generates a positive cash flow until you have enough monthly income equal to or greater than the income from your job. Once that happens, you can tell your boss to kiss off.

You Don't Need As Much Money As You Made From Your Job

You don't need to make the same amount of money from your commercial real estate investments, as you do from your job. Your commercial real estate investments only need to net enough money to replace the income you brought home each month. For instance, if you were earning $4,000 per month from your job, and after taxes you brought home $3,000 per month, your goal would be to purchase enough commercial real estate to generate a monthly positive cash flow of $3,000. If you had to accomplish this with residential real estate, it may take purchasing 30-50 homes to reach your goal. That's a lot of real estate to keep track of. With commercial real estate, that could easily be accomplished with only one property.

But, of course, you don't want to just make the same amount of money as you do with your job. You want to make a lot more money than that. Whatever your goal is-whether it is $5,000, $10,000, or $100,000 positive monthly cash flow-hold off on any speculation deals until you've reached your financial goal. Once you know that not only all your monthly bills are paid, but you are financially set for life, then you will be in a better financial position to do more speculative real estate investments. Don't gamble, until you can afford to do so.

WORKING FROM HOME IS OVER RATED

Many infomercials feature people saying, "I work from home, just a few hours per week! I now have more time with my family." While it's true that you may spend more time at home, it doesn't necessarily mean that you will spend more time with your family. Being physically present at home may mean that your work gets half the attention it should, while your family gets half the attention they should.

Your Family May Not Understand That You Have A "Real" Job

Our computer is located in our kitchen area. While working, I'm physically present, but completely concentrating on my task at hand. My husband, Mike, will come into the kitchen and start a conversation with me, or shall I say, he tries to have a conversation with me. At that point, I have two choices:

1. Stop and really listen to what he has to say, or
2. Half listen while I continue to work-which seems to be the one I usually choose.

Later on, when I ask Mike a question he'll say, "I told you about that earlier today." If I do stop to fully listen to him, then I have to find my work zone again, only to be distracted ten minutes later by one of my boys wanting a cup of juice.

I can't even tell you the number of times when I'm conducting business on the telephone and it's like my boys have a special radar that instantly causes them to increase their yelling and screaming. My mortgage broker hears all of the noise in the background (which I'm now deaf to) and he tells me, "I don't know how you do it."

Working from home has been a tough transition. It took a while for Mike to understand that just like a "real" job, I need to work everyday (I take one day off each week). I need a good five to six hours per day to get what I need done, done.

Working On Your Own Terms

It's not working from home that has the appeal for most people, rather working on your own terms, that is the true desire. I love that I can schedule an appointment at any hour of the day. I love that I can lay down if I'm tired and take a nap with my boys. I love the freedom of working all morning and then finally getting into the shower at 1:00 PM or heck, skipping the shower all together. I love the fact that I make the decisions and answer only to myself. I love the fact that all of my efforts will make my family rich instead of increasing the wealth of another corporation.

Missing Adult Interaction

I really do miss the daily interaction with people though. My big outing of the day usually consists of going to the gym (very important for the mental stress of commercial real estate investing). I may be lucky enough to meet some friendly people at the park with the kids. I even find going to a doctor appointment by myself relaxing.

Even with all the draw backs of working from home, it still

beats the ol' 9-5, hands down, all day long. Just know, that the transition may be more difficult than it looks.

TEAM MEMBERS

Find Them As You Go

A lot of real estate investing books I've read emphasize the importance for real estate investors to network and build a team. I agree with that. Where I disagree, is that you should establish your team before you begin investing in commercial real estate. You would be spending so much time trying to establish a team, that you wouldn't have any time to find any properties. Establish your contacts and find team members as you go.

A good example of this was with my condo conversion project. I went into the project not having one team member selected. Honestly, I didn't even know who I needed on my team. The city couldn't help me out with any references either because they had never had a condo conversion application before. I found Rey Berona (www.rberona.com), a condo conversion consultant, through The Creative Investor website (www.thecreativeinvestor.com). I emailed Rey and asked him if he would be willing to help me when I got stuck, as I didn't have anyone else I could turn to.

He agreed to help me and immediately gave me the contact information for almost every condo conversion professional I would need. He gave me the name of an attorney to draft the CC&R's, the name of a CPA to prepare the association's budget and reserve study, the name of a civil engineer who could prepare the condominium plan, and the name of the title company that specializes in condo conversions. He knew these people did a good job. If I had tried to find all of these team members before I started the condominium conversion project, I would not have found people with specific condo conversion experience on my own.

Your Team Members Will Change

You are about to get into much more sophisticated real estate transactions. As you expand into these larger commercial real estate properties the professionals you need as members of your team will change. You may realize that the person you have been working with is no longer suitable for your needs.

For example, you will need the services of a commercial real estate agent instead of a residential real estate agent. Or you may find yourself needing the services of a more sophisticated real estate attorney who is familiar with commercial real estate transactions at the level you are on. For instance, I wouldn't work with the same caliber of attorney Donald Trump uses. His attorneys are used to working with the legalities of the complex real estate transactions he's involved in.

If you keep your existing team members that you have been using for your residential real estate investing needs, they may render advice that is actually incorrect or harmful. This situation happened to me when I purchased my first commercial property. My real estate agent had advised me to have the purchase contract reviewed by a real estate attorney. I hadn't previously needed the services of a real estate attorney, so I wasn't quite sure what qualities to look for. I had asked for a recommendation from a few people, but found that recommendations were lacking. I knew I wanted to sit down with an attorney who also invested in real estate, thinking he would have first hand knowledge of certain situations I would need to be cautious about. After several calls, I found an attorney, and set up an appointment.

When I met with the attorney, he looked at the purchase contract only from a legality point of view. I was expecting some great words of wisdom from him like, "Watch out for this inspection contingency time frame because if you go past it, you will not get your earnest money back." But no, I received nothing of the sort. His only response was, "Everything looks legal." Well yes, Mr. Attorney, almost anything written on a piece of paper which is signed between two parties is legal. I already knew that. He then suggested to me that the best investment strategy was to hold onto the property long term and to pay it off as quickly as possible. That was the nail in his coffin. A paid off property is not a smart move, financially, or from an asset protection point of view either. This guy did not know what he was talking about.

They Can't Know Everything

There's another thing I want to discuss with you regarding "professionals." You shouldn't depend upon them to know everything they should know. For instance, you can't assume that a CPA knows everything there is to know about real estate deductions. A CPA knows the most common tax deductions, but he can't know them all. You need to continually educate yourself because the tax laws constantly change.

Find out how many of your CPA's clients own commercial real estate. It probably won't be many. Last year, my CPA told me that my tax return was one of his most complicated. It looks like I will have to find a new CPA soon.

My point with all of this is to let you know that your team members will constantly change. Be aware of this. Also, do not be concerned if you don't have all of your team members assembled prior to needing them. You will find them as you go.

WHAT NOBODY TELLS YOU

1. Commercial real estate is a great investment now and will continue to be in the future.
2. There will come a point when serious residential real estate investors will almost be forced to move up to investing in commercial real estate.
3. Purchasing real estate with negative cash flow is not investing, but a form of insanity called speculation.
4. You can know where future developments are coming before anyone else does.
5. Positive cash flow is king, until you are so wealthy that you can afford to gamble by speculation.
6. Working from home isn't as glorious as portrayed on infomercials. However, working on your own terms is.
7. Don't worry about finding all of your team members at once.
8. Bad advice can cost you big time!

CHAPTER 4
GETTING STARTED
(FINALLY)

You have stuck through my "words of wisdom." It's now time to get into the detailed steps of investing in commercial real estate. The very first step of investing in commercial real estate, you are actually doing right now. You are getting yourself educated.

LACK OF KNOWLEDGE CAN BE A LIFE OR DEATH SITUATION

My son, Camden, was swimming in the pool one day. My other son, Connor, and I were watching Camden swim. Connor hadn't quite taken to the pool yet. At the time, he just enjoyed playing with his toys outside while watching his brother swim. Well, Connor decided to start walking around the perimeter of the pool. "Connor," I said. "Stop walking around the pool. You're going to fall in. Move away from the edge of the pool." Of course, as any two year old would, he completely ignored his mother. Sure enough, he lost his balance and fell into the pool. I was in there, not more than one second later, fishing him out.

For one son, the pool was a source of delight and play. For my other son, it could have been deadly. It made me realize that the only difference between their two experiences was KNOWLEDGE. Although it was the same pool, one child had knowledge of how to swim, while the other child didn't. The difference in their level of knowledge made their experience of the same pool, vastly different. Your experience investing in commercial real estate is the same way. It can be a lot of fun or it can be an awful experience, depending upon how much knowledge you have.

IT DOESN'T MATTER WHAT KIND OF FINANCIAL ENVIRONMENT YOU GREW UP IN

My husband and I have always had opposite investment styles. I am the aggressive one, while he is the conservative one. I find the difference of our investment styles fascinating because we grew up in completely opposite financial environments. Mike's family was financially well off. While we always had enough food and clothes, my family didn't have a lot of money to spend on the "extras." When I was growing up, I remember thinking that if I ever made $50,000/year, I would be financially set.

Experiencing my family's financial situation as a child, motivated me to do whatever was necessary to accomplish financial independence. I didn't grow up with money, but I have educated myself about money and investing through countless hours of reading. Mike grew up in a family with money, but was never specifically taught how to make money work for him. Once he went out on his own, he was financially unprepared, and failed to reach his full financial potential.

Your prior knowledge about money, or lack thereof, is not an indication of your ability to get yourself educated and on the right financial track, NOW.

COLLEGE ISN'T YOUR ONLY OPTION

I believe everyone should get an education. However, I'm not talking about going through the "traditional" educational path of attending college. In fact, unless there is a specific profession that requires the college route, such as a doctor or dentist, I would skip college all together. I'm sure I'm going to ruffle a lot of feathers by saying that.

Statistically, you will find that those people who have had the greatest financial success in the past, made their money by starting their own business or through real estate ownership. Bypassing the traditional college route may save you a lot of time and money which you could use to start a business or invest in real estate.

Pencil It Out

I was fortunate that becoming a dental hygienist took only four years of college. The ability to earn $60,000/year straight out of college, is not common with most professions. During the course of my dental hygiene profession, many people asked me why I didn't go back to school to become a dentist.

The reason was because it just didn't pencil out. It wasn't a smart financial move. To become a dentist, I would need another year of college to take the classes needed to apply to dental school. Then, it would take an additional four years to complete dental school. Adding together the cost of dental school, at a minimum price of $100,000 to the cost of my lost wages as a dental hygienist for five years, ($80,000/year at the time) the true cost for me to become a dentist would be $500,000. If I took that $500,000 I would have spent becoming a dentist, and invested it instead, after 30 years I would easily have over $5,000,000 (8% rate of return assumed). Was going to dental school really worth it? No way!

Times Have Changed

There is no better substitute for teaching than real life experience. When you first started investing in real estate, you received the best education there was, which was learning by doing it-figuring out what worked and didn't work along the way. The best learning experiences do not happen in a classroom, rather by real-life experience, in your chosen field.

"Formal education will make you a living. Self education will make you a fortune."
- Jim Rohn

Even traditional business colleges that "teach" entrepreneurship, are usually taught by teachers who may not even be entrepreneurs themselves. You want to learn your chosen profession from someone who is already doing what it is you would like to do and is incredibly brilliant at it.

We live in a different age today. If you refuse to adapt to today's environment, and stay with the "go to high school, then to college, then get a good corporate job" mentality, financially you will be left behind. I'm not saying that you won't have a nice comfortable life, but I am saying that you won't be living up to your true financial potential that way.

Parents, do you want to see your kids financially average? It is true that in the past getting a college degree was the best financial move to make. Now, that's rarely the case.

Don't Waste Your Brilliance

There's nothing more frustrating than to see the brilliance of a person, when they don't see it in themself. We've all witnessed this before. You see someone who is a genius in a certain area, yet they settle for a job for it's "security."

I thought about this just the other day while I was watching American Idol. Most of the people on the show who eventually end up in the finals had ordinary jobs, like working in a bank or at a car part store before they joined the show. These people have incredible talent and the really scary part is the thought that if American Idol hadn't come to the United States, they would still be working in those ordinary jobs, letting their amazing talent go to waste.

Life is not a dress rehearsal. There are no retakes. If you consciously *settle* for a comfortable, average life for the "security" of a job, you may live with regret later in life.

It is impossible to know everything about commercial real estate investing, but you can, and should, do some preliminary studying to help guide you down the right path. Let's take a

51

look at some potential ways to start your self education.

READ LIKE A MAD DOG

Books

Your local library should be your best friend. You should read like a mad dog about all aspects of real estate investing. Although current commercial real estate investing books are lacking (not counting this one, of course), there are some aspects of residential real estate investing that will carry over to the commercial side. Most of you have probably read *Rich Dad, Poor Dad,* by Robert Kiyosaki. If you haven't, then you must start there. It's a quick read and will change the way you think about money and investing. Another author, Ty Hicks, although not quite as well known as Robert Kiyosaki, has written some great real estate investing books as well!

There are literally hundreds, if not thousands, of superb books available to read. I usually pick up three to five books from the library every two weeks. That's why the library is so great! I would spend a fortune if I bought all of the books I read. I like to read while I work out, so I can get educated and fit, at the same time. Reading three books in two weeks may be a bit much for you, but reading two books a month is not an unrealistic goal at all.

Newspapers

Current events are important to keep up on. There may be items in your local paper that are important to know about because it may affect your commercial real estate investment opportunities. For instance, if you read that a major company is relocating to Indiana, that will affect the surrounding area with an increase in the population size. The increased population size will cause a higher demand for businesses and housing to accommodate the new residents, causing existing real estate prices to increase. Or, perhaps a hurricane affected area may present you with an opportunity to purchase real estate at a drastically discounted price.

If you decide to not take my advice of keeping up with the local developments by watching your city's planning commission and city council meetings, then the newspaper will apprise you of new developments, but at a later date than you could have gotten the information yourself.

Remember, that the media can slant news stories anyway they like. Good news doesn't sell newspapers. So, be careful when you read real estate related articles because the information may, or may not to true. For instance, if you read that real estate sales are soft, that does not mean it's true for every single area in the United States. Real estate prices are affected by many, many things.

The more you keep up with current events, the better decisions you can make.

Magazines

Millionaire Blueprints, Forbes, Entrepreneur, Fortune. I love them all! Sometimes you will find an article in a magazine that will spark an idea for a property you currently own or for a property you would have normally overlooked. For instance, I once read an article that reported the top ten cities to start a business. Don't you think that information would be important to know? Would you be able to use that information to look for real estate for sale in those areas, especially if appreciation is an important factor for you?

Another article featured information about high-end manufactured homes. What if you were able to find subdivided land on which you could put these high-end manufactured homes, completing a development in 1/10th of the normal time frame? That's an idea. Another article was about high-end, climate controlled, condominiums that wealthy people can purchase to store their luxury cars.

The magazine articles don't even have to be directly related to commercial real estate investing for them to be useful to you. For example, I read an article about a new machine which stores electricity when it's the cheapest rate and then uses the stored electricity during peak rates, causing the property owner's electricity expense to significantly decrease.

All of these examples I used above, are actual articles I have clipped out. In magazines you can also read incredible stories about other entrepreneurs who have overcome many obstacles on their journey to success. When you read about the struggles and eventual success of others, it will inspire you to continue working towards your own goals. Most successful people are successful because they have worked incredibly hard.

SEMINARS

The Learning Annex

I love, love, love seminars. Did I already mention that I love seminars? The biggest and best one going right now for real estate investors is The Learning Annex Real Estate Wealth Expo. I was actually featured in an infomercial they produced as a "success story." This seminar is put on in various cities across the country featuring the biggest and most popular keynote speakers, such as Donald Trump, Robert Kiyosaki, and Tony Robbins. No wonder they draw crowds of 40,000-60,000 people! It is just a great place to open your mind to ideas about investing in the various niches of real estate, such as wholeselling, foreclosures, probate properties, and yes, even commercial real estate.

At The Learning Annex Real Estate Wealth Expo various featured speakers give a one to three hour presentation about their particular subject, and then invite you to purchase their course. I usually buy one or two courses each time I go. They run anywhere from $500-$12,000. Whenever I let someone know how much money I paid for a course, their eyes get all big and with disbelief they'll ask me, "How can you spend so much money on that?"

> Why is it acceptable in our society for a person to spend four to six years in college, accumulating over $50,000 in debt to earn $30,000 per year, yet it's not acceptable for someone to spend $1,000 for a five day boot camp and course, which provides the information that allows someone to potentially make over $100,000 per year?

Why is it acceptable in our society for a person to spend four to six years in college, accumulating over $50,000 in debt to earn $30,000 per year, yet it's not acceptable for someone to spend $1,000 for a five day boot camp and course, which provides the information that allows someone to potentially make over $100,000 per year? The logic is bizarre.

With the information I learned from one course I purchased, I did a deal that took four months to complete, which netted me $36,000. As a bonus, once I learn the information from the course, I sell it on eBay and usually receive about half the cost of the course back. It's a win-win situation. I get part of my investment back, while someone else gets the course at a highly discounted rate. Try getting half your money back after you take a college course.

What kind of return did I get on my educational investment? A phenomenal one! Is $1,000 a lot of money to spend on a real estate investing course? It's all depends upon your perspective.

Your Friends May Change

Seminars are a also great place to network and find like-minded people. You may have already experienced, being the motivated person you are, feeling out of sorts with most of your peers. At my age, there is hardly anyone I know of who has the same ambitious goals as I have. It can get lonely. When you have success, there can be a lot of jealousy and many friendships can't be sustained because of it.

Just as you may have to change your team members, you may also have to change friends too. You will need to find friends who are at least on the same level as you, or higher. Not financially per say, but at least in their drive, goals, motivation level, and dreams. Attending seminars is so refreshing because everyone else is just like you. They want to be successful. They are ambitious and dedicated. It is truly refreshing to meet people who think the way you do.

ONLINE

The Creative Investor

There is a real estate website that I consider to be the absolutely best online resource for getting yourself educated about investing in commercial real estate. It is The Creative Investor (www.thecreativeinvestor.com). This website has informative articles and forums with knowledgeable people who can answer your questions about investing in commercial real estate. In the forums you can find questions asked by other novice commercial real estate investors on just about every commercial real estate topic you could think of. You can even run the numbers of a particular property by other commercial real estate investors to get their input about the viability of a certain deal.

The Creative Investor website is how I came into contact with Rey Berona. As I mentioned before, Rey is a condo conversion expert, who helped me for free on my condo conversion project in Redding, California. "Actually, it wasn't for free." he clarified. "I charged her a cup of coffee." I was blown away that he would do that for me. What a great asset to have! Thank goodness for The Creative Investor.

There may be certain topics that you want more in-depth information about. In that case, all you need to do is type the topic into an internet search engine and read until your heart's content. The internet has leveled the playing field for residential real estate investors who want to step up to investing in commercial real estate, by allowing anyone who wants information, to have access to it.

No matter which way you get yourself educated, the point is to do it. You should consistently be striving to learn more and more. You will never know everything. What fun would that be anyway?

WHAT NOBODY TELLS YOU

1. It's up to you to get educated and stay educated.
2. Traditional college prepares you for a job, which will not make you wealthy.
3. You should never stop learning.
4. Nobody knows everything, nor ever will.
5. The internet is an unlimited source of information.
6. If you ask, people will help you.
7. Find friends who will support your goals and dreams, as being ambitious can get lonely.
8. Current events affect your real estate investing opportunities.

CHAPTER 5
FINDING COMMERCIAL PROPERTIES

The hunt is on. You are ready to go. You are excited. Let's discuss where and how to find commercial real estate for sale.

SOME MARKETS ARE EASIER THAN OTHERS

If you happen to go to a real estate investing seminar, you will find that most speakers will say you can work their system anywhere in the country. That may be true. What isn't true, though, is that all areas are equal. Some areas are a lot easier for novice commercial real estate investors to purchase commercial real estate than other areas. This is because of the cost factor. Purchasing commercial real estate requires a larger down payment than purchasing residential real estate does, and let's face it, the major obstacle of purchasing real estate, is finding the money for the down payment. The combination of the higher purchase price and the higher down payment required, makes stepping up to investing in commercial real estate extremely difficult in certain areas such as California, New York, or Las Vegas.

For instance, here in Las Vegas, there are a ton of real estate investors who have deep pockets. When a real estate auction is held, there will be literally over one thousand people present for a chance to bid on just a couple of properties. The property is sold to the highest bidder-a bid which is based from only a drive-by of the property's exterior-with it's interior sight unseen. The successful bidder must pay for the property, in full, by the end of the day. Most of the auctioned homes are sold for above it's market value.

> It is very common to find apartment buildings priced at less than $30,000 per unit. That's the price of an average car.

I always joke that if you want to sell your house in Las Vegas in a couple of years, then you shouldn't pay your property taxes. The county will sell your house at a property tax sale, where you could almost be guaranteed that the house would sell for above market value. As an added bonus, you would not have to pay a commission to a real estate agent. I am just kidding of course, but it's that crazy here.

However, if you go to Ohio, it's a whole different scenario. They hold property auctions every week. Most of the time, the bank takes the property back because it's not bought at auction.

The location in which you seek to invest, *does* make a difference as to how easy, or difficult, it is to start investing in commercial real estate. That doesn't mean that if you live in an expensive area, such as California, you have an excuse. It really shouldn't matter where you live, as the internet allows anyone around the world to access commercial real estate for sale in areas that are reasonably priced.

Midwest States Are Easier To Find Suitable Properties

Purchasing properties located in the Midwest states seems to be an easier place for novice commercial real estate investors to start. These states will have more commercial properties for sale that have the positive cash flow you are seeking, at prices that are unbelievably low. It is very common to find apartment buildings priced for less than $30,000 per unit. That's the price of an average car right now. With the increase in land prices and with skyrocketing construction costs, I just can't see how the price of the properties located in the Midwest can go down any further than they are right now.

Many large corporations are starting to see the benefit of moving to the Midwest states as well because their two largest operating costs-lease payments and labor-can be greatly reduced. As we all know, corporations are all about the money. The savings are too great to pass up. Most states fight hard to get corporations to relocate to their state, by offering economic incentives and property tax waivers. Watch for the corporate relocation trend to continue in the future as well.

I have been paying particularly close attention to Ohio because that is where I own 57 apartment units. It seems that Ohio's economy has been in shambles for a while. Part of the problem has been that every single state surrounding Ohio allows Indian gaming, financially benefitting from that fact.

The residents of Ohio have voted down Indian gaming

numerous times before. However, with Ohio's currently poor economic situation, it's residents are realizing that they need to do something. It looks like Indian gaming *may* be in Ohio's future. Whether that happens or not, with inflation and rising constructions costs, the price of real estate in Ohio just can't be beat.

YOU MUST HAVE A CRITERIA

Before a pilot takes off, he knows where he is going. If his destination is Florida, then he better have that destination entered into the plane's computer. If he enters in Canada as his

> **Yet, real estate investors do this all the time. They just start randomly looking at investment properties wondering, *Is this a good deal?* The answer all depends upon how you define a good deal.**

destination, he certainly won't end up in Florida. What if he didn't enter in any destination at all and just decided to take off? He would be hard pressed to find either Florida or Canada. Yet, real estate investors do this all the time. They just start randomly looking at investment properties wondering, *Is this a good deal?*

The answer all depends upon how you define a good deal. What is your destination? Are you looking for a property with positive cash flow? Are you looking for a property that will rapidly appreciate? Are you looking for an apartment building that is suitable to convert to condominiums? Before you actually start looking for commercial real estate to purchase, you must establish a criteria. You must know what you are looking for. Only then can the question, "Is this a good deal?" be answered.

Let's say you take my advice and decide to look for an apartment building to purchase as your first commercial real estate investment. That is your first criteria. If you are looking for apartment buildings, you don't need to waste your time looking at other types of commercial real estate, such as retail centers.

Then, you decide that the property must generate a cash on cash return of no less than 10%. Your criteria is narrowed even more. What is left, is a nice group of properties that meets your minimum criteria, which you will analyze further. Remember, you want to look for positive cash flowing properties, until you get to the point where you can say goodbye to your J-O-B.

My primary criteria for a property I plan to keep long term is that it must provide me with a minimum of a 20% cash on cash return. A *cash on cash return* is the annual net income of the property, (debt service included) divided by the amount of money you put into the property, as a down payment.

For instance, if you put down $100,000 on a property which netted $20,000/year, that is a 20% cash on cash return. Here's how it is calculated:

$$\frac{\$20,000 \text{ Annual Net Profit}}{\$100,000 \text{ Money You Have In The Deal}} = 20\% \text{ Cash On Cash Return}$$

Many people have told me that finding a property that provides a 20% cash on cash return is an unreasonable expectation. I agree that it's not easy to find, but it can be done. My first commercial property I bought in Ohio, generated a 26% cash on cash return for me the first year I owned it.

If you are looking solely for appreciation, (and you better not be) it is a bit more difficult to establish a criteria. Essentially, you would have to make an educated guess, based upon the previous appreciation level for the area. We have already discussed the strategies that will help you make better choices, if you choose to invest-I mean speculate-this way.

If you are looking for an apartment building to convert to condominiums, the cash on cash return would be irrelevant. You would be looking at the price per unit instead.

Can you see the importance of establishing your criteria before you embark on this journey? I always thought that if more people set a criteria for their future spouse, it would make dating a whole lot easier! Ladies, if you want to date a man who is at least 5'7", doesn't smoke, and has brown hair, why waste your time dating a man who is 5'5", smokes, and has blond hair? I may be over simplifying it though!

Don't get sidetracked by properties (or men, for that matter) that don't meet the specific parameters you have established ahead of time. Just say ....NEXT!

WHERE TO LOOK?

I wouldn't go to any night clubs, as they are just meat markets.

Ohhh, I'm sorry. We're back to talking about commercial real estate investing. That makes it much easier then!

The Internet

Back in the day, before you were playing in the real estate big leagues, if you were looking to purchase a residential investment property, you would most likely look on the Multiple Listing Service (MLS). You could look in the newspaper, drive around, and check online as well. But generally, your best bet for finding a residential investment property would be by accessing the MLS.

The crappy thing is, that only real estate agents/brokers can access the MLS. You can't sit in the comfort of your home and access that specific information anytime you wanted to, unless you could find a real estate agent who is willing to give you their password, and risk being severally fined. So, what normally happens is that the real estate agent will ask you for certain parameters, and then forward to you those listings that meet the parameters.

Let me give you an example of why this would be a problem. Imagine saying this to a residential real estate agent:

"Please forward to me any listing that is a 3 bedroom, 2 bathroom home, located on a golf course, priced under $300,000, with a tenant in place, that rents for a minimum of $3,000/month, where the seller is willing to carry a second mortgage, and the existing mortgage can be assumed."

She would either just look at you, or laugh. On top of that, real estate agents can't search for listings nationwide, which really limits a real estate investor from finding a lot of

Chapter Five

exceptional deals.

Loopnet

In your search to purchase commercial properties, it's a much easier process. My favorite place to look for commercial real estate for sale is on a website called Loopnet (www.loopnet.com). They *so* owe me big time for referring so many people to their website, but I digress.

Okay, Loopnet is *the* place to look for commercial real estate for sale. Every single one of the commercial properties I have purchased, I found by searching on Loopnet. It is the largest online commercial real estate listing service in the nation. All across the country, commercial real estate agents and brokers from companies such as ReMax Commercial, CBRE, Century 21 Commercial, and Coldwell Banker, list all of the commercial properties they have for sale or lease on Loopnet. Property owners can list their commercial property for sale or lease on Loopnet as well. Try doing that on the MLS!

Loopnet's basic membership is free, but you will not be able to access all of the listings unless you become a "premium" member. Loopnet's premium membership costs $59.95/month (as of writing this). Now, I know that a premium membership may seem like an unnecessary expense to pay. Here's my logic on it though.

Let's say there's a listing on Loopnet that you can't access, because you didn't want to spend the $59.95/month for the premium membership. That property, if you had been able to view it and then purchased it, would have brought in $20,000/year more than any other property you were able to view. However, because you were too cheap to pay the extra

$720/year to view all of the listings on Loopnet, you lost out on $20,000 every single year you would have owned the property. That doesn't make a whole lot of sense to me.

Being frugal is good. Being cheap is not. If you are serious about investing in commercial real estate, pay for Loopnet's premium membership to get access to all of the listings.

eBay

The other place that you can look for commercial properties for sale is on eBay. I actually found a commercial property on eBay, locked it up with a purchase contract, but wasn't able to get the financing in place to close the deal. When a property is posted on the internet, the entire world (anybody with an internet connection) can see it. It's great for both buyers and sellers. Buyers have more commercial properties to choose from and sellers have more potential buyers looking at their commercial property for sale.

Auction Websites

There are many other websites, such as Tranzon (www.tranzon.com), that auctions commercial real estate, but I wanted to focus on those websites that you would use the majority of the time.

BUSINESSES FOR SALE

Split The Business From The Real Estate

Many times, a business that includes real estate will be listed for sale by a business broker. While you may not be interested in owning a business, you may be able to make this work for you. Most business owners don't want to own real estate. If you find a business for sale that includes the real estate, why not put a call into the business broker to let him know you may be interested in purchasing the real estate, if the business owner is willing to sign a new lease (written in your favor of course). It gives the property owner and business broker more options. They may be bombarded by calls from people who are interested in purchasing the business, but not the real estate.

Let's do an example of this. Let's say that you purchased a car dealership for $3,000,000 named "ABC Car Sales," which includes the real estate. There is no existing lease in place, as the tenant and the landlord are the same company. After the business is officially yours, you then establish a company named "ABC Real Estate," which will be the new owner of the building. If you execute a new long term, NNN lease agreement (See Chapter 6 about different types of leases.) between ABC Car Sales and ABC Real Estate for $350,000/year, then you would have increased the value of the real estate by $500,000 (at a 10% cap rate). Once the new lease is in place, you could then sell the business off separately, for $500,000, keeping the real estate for yourself.

Let's see how splitting the business from the real estate can make a large difference to your net worth.

OLD VALUE   **NEW VALUE**

Business and Real   Business $500,000
Estate Combined $3,000,000   Real Estate $3,500,000

Total   **$3,000,000**   **$4,000,000**

With a couple of hours of work, you have increased your net worth by $1,000,000. We will go over calculating commercial real estate values in Chapter 7. At this point, just keep in mind that this scenario is a possibility.

BUSINESSES NOT FOR SALE

Find Business Owners Who Need Cash

Many cash strapped, business owners own the real estate in which they operate their business. There may be a large amount of equity in their property that they would like to access, but aren't quite sure how to go about it. They probably don't want to go through the hassle of marketing their property for sale, with a large FOR SALE sign in front of their business, that could scare their employees and clients-so they stay with the situation as it is.

If you were able to find those businesses owners, who own the real estate associated with their business, they may be extremely receptive to selling their property to you, simultaneously executing a new long term lease agreement. Because you will have the knowledge of what the property is worth once the lease agreement is signed, you should be able to secure unbelievable bargains. The term used for this type of transaction is a "Sale-Leaseback."

Whether you are looking to purchase commercial properties that are listed for sale, or not, you need to maintain your previously established criteria at all times.

Chapter Five

WHAT NOBODY TELLS YOU

1. Making the transition from investing in residential real estate to investing in commercial real estate is easier in some area than other areas.

2. You must have a criteria. If you don't know what you're looking for, you won't find it.

3. Your criteria should be different for each type of property, depending upon what you want to do with it.

4.Commercial real estate listings are easier to access than residential real estate listings.

5. Loopnet is the best place to look for commercial real estate that is for sale or lease.

6. Business owners and business brokers are untapped resources for finding commercial real estate deals.

ANALYZING COMMERCIAL REAL ESTATE

This chapter is going to be quite in depth. You may want to grab a snack to make sure you are mentally geared up for all this information. You have set a criteria that will work for you. You are ready to look for commercial properties on Loopnet that will fit your criteria. When analyzing a commercial property, there are many, many, factors to consider. If a specific section pertains to primarily one type of commercial real estate, I will have that information under it's appropriate heading, such as **RETAIL, OFFICE,** or **APARTMENTS**. Let's begin.

LOCATION, LOCATION, LOCATION

You Don't Have To Live Or Work There

When analyzing a commercial property, please remember to keep your personal standards out of the picture. The purchase of a residential property that you will personally live in is an emotional decision. Emotions shouldn't come into play when purchasing commercial real estate. This is a business. You are seeking to make the best rate of return possible from your investment. Your primary concern should be whether or not the property in question meets your previously established criteria.

Location Is Not A Huge Factor In The Value Of A Commercial Property

Commercial real estate's value is not based upon "comps" or comparable properties like residential real estate. It's value is based strictly upon how much money the property generates. Period. It doesn't matter if it is as ugly as sin, located in the ghetto, with graffiti all over it. Pretty properties, located in the "nice" part of town, may not generate as much money for you as the ugly properties located in the "bad" part of town.

Out Of State Is Great

Don't be afraid to invest in commercial real estate that is located out of state. You will miss out on a lot of great properties if you are not willing to venture out of your local area. We are not living in the horse and buggy era. You can be across the country in four hours. That does not mean you will be flying all over the country, looking at dozens of commercial properties. That would be a big waste of time and money. You will have a property locked up with a purchase contract before you ever fly out to the property to perform an inspection (more on that to come).

Don't Purchase Real Estate Located Out Of Country, For Now

When you are making the transition from investing in residential real estate, to investing in commercial real estate, you shouldn't consider purchasing properties located outside of this country. There are just too many unknown elements which raises it's risk level. There's plenty of real estate investment opportunities here, in the good ol' USA, to risk dealing with other country's laws and regulations. Once you have completed a few commercial deals, then you can evaluate whether or not you feel educated enough to make an out of country real estate investment choice.

> Be cautious if you see a year after year decrease in the population. There's generally a reason why. It's hard to fill vacancies when everyone's leaving.

DEMOGRAPHICS

Which Way Is The Population Size Heading?

Find out not only the current population size of the city and county where the property is located, but which direction the population size is heading. Loopnet has a button under "Options," which gives you access to the demographics of an area surrounding a specific property. A steady increase in the population size, or at a minimum maintaining it's current population size, is a plus. Be cautious if you see a year after year decrease in the population size. There's generally a reason why. It's hard to fill vacancies when everyone's leaving.

What Is The Surrounding Household Income?

RETAIL

The property's current and future tenants should correspond to the household income levels surrounding the property. Do you think that a Neiman Marcus store will be located in an area which has an average household income of $20,000? If it is, it won't be there for long. Lenders love to see high income neighborhoods surrounding retail developments.

APARTMENTS

The household income level surrounding the property, should reflect in the rental rates of apartments as well. If half the population of a city is earning less than $10,000/year, and each apartment unit rents for $1,000/month, the low percentage of people in the population who can afford that rental amount will make renting vacant units tough.

What Is The Ethnic Make-Up Of The Surrounding Area?

This is not a discriminatory thing. You should not look at a particular ethnicity as good or bad thing. It's just another factor in your decision of whether or not you decide to purchase a particular building. You will need to know who the current tenants are, as well as who your potential future tenants will be. Doing so, will enable you to purchase a property that can accommodate your prospective tenants more

74

effectively.

RETAIL

Do you see that 90% of the population surrounding the property is Hispanic? Then you will need to find a property management company that can speak Spanish. You will also target vacancies towards businesses that cater to that specific community.

APARTMENTS

The Hispanic community is the fastest growing ethnicity group in the United States. The Hispanic community tends to have larger than average sized families. Purchasing an apartment building located within a largely Hispanic community that only has studio or one bedroom units, may result in larger than expected vacancy levels.

OCCUPANCY LEVEL

If There Is A Vacancy, It May Be Difficult To Find A New Tenant

RETAIL

Everyone needs a place to live, but not everyone owns a business. It's just common knowledge that it takes much longer for a vacant office or retail space to be filled with a replacement tenant, than it takes for a vacant apartment unit to be filled with a tenant. This is particularly true if the rental space is over 2,500 Sq Ft. There are not a lot of business owners who need to rent spaces larger than that size. Protect yourself by not purchasing a property that has a lot of large retail or office spaces, unless they can be divided into smaller spaces.

Anchor Tenants Are Important

If the anchor tenant space is vacant, that is a big problem. The smaller businesses that are in the same development, depend upon the volume of traffic that an anchor tenant brings to the property. Without one, it's usually just a matter of time before the other businesses start closing their doors, leaving you with even more vacancies.

> The property may have a great occupancy level now, but if the leases are going to expire soon, you would be paying for the property at a higher price, but have the risk associated with the future vacancies. This is not good!

Watch For Impending Vacancies

I always find it comical when a property owner lists his commercial property for sale a year or so before one of the main tenant's lease is set to expire. Why would anybody buy a commercial property knowing that it's going to be vacant in a year or two? The property may have a great occupancy level now, but if the leases are going to expire soon, you would be paying for the property at a higher price, but have the risk associated with the future vacancies. This is not good! To make the situation even worse, you would have to be financially prepared to pay leasing commissions which could prove costly.

I think it would be more wise for a property owner to sell his commercial property a couple of years after a new lease is executed, when the property's value can't be disputed due to an impending vacancy.

APARTMENTS

If you will need to obtain traditional commercial lender financing, the property's occupancy better be at a minimum level of 80% (20% vacancy). Sometimes a lower occupancy level is acceptable to the lender if you can provide a sufficient explanation, such as poor property management or the death of the property owner. The lender will verify the occupancy level from the property's rent roll and lease agreements when you get to that point.

Use Standard Vacancy Levels

On the other hand, if a property is 100% occupied, there's know where for it's income to go, but down. For this reason, you should use a standard vacancy level of 5-10% when calculating a property's financial potential even if the property is currently 100% occupied. Doing so, will help you create a realistic picture of the property's financial potential. Additionally, this is how a commercial real estate lender will calculate the property's vacancy level. You want to ensure that there will not be a problem in obtaining financing because you were painting too rosy of a picture of the property's financial potential.

Rent Guarantees Can Help In Negotiations With A Seller

Sometimes a seller will offer the purchaser a rent guarantee for a certain period of time. This concession may be used to give the property a higher value or allow the purchaser time to fill larger than normal vacancy levels. If this concession is not offered by the seller, you can still ask for it. It's a great compromise when a seller is stuck on a asking price that is just too high based upon the property's existing vacancy level. Don't forget to factor into the purchase price the fact that you will have to pay leasing commissions for those vacancies to be filled as well.

EXISTING TENANTS

When you purchase investment real estate, you will be obligated to take over all the existing leases associated with the property with their existing provisions. You must make sure you know to what you are agreeing. Usually, you will not be able to review the actual lease agreements until you are in contract to purchase the property. However, the seller's listing agent will supply you with some information to start your evaluation such as, who the main tenants are, the property's existing occupancy level, and the property's rent roll.

Are The Tenant's Rental Rates Where They Should Be?

RETAIL/OFFICE

Are the tenant's rental rates below, at, or above market rental rates? To find out, you will need to go on Loopnet once more. This time, you will search under "Properties For Lease," not "Properties For Sale." Find several comparable properties within a three mile radius of the subject property, to compare what their rental rates are.

When comparing rental rates, make sure you are comparing

apples to apples. You want to ensure that the size of the rental space, the property's age and class are similar. Let's say that the property you are looking to purchase is 5,000 Sq Ft and has a yearly income of $30,000. After doing your homework, you find out that the market rental rate of comparable properties is $10/Sq Ft or $50,000/year (5,000 Sq Ft X $10/Sq Ft). In this case, the tenant's rental rate of $30,000/year is way below the market rental rate.

If the tenant's rental rate is below market rental rates, it could be advantageous for you because you will purchase the property for a price based upon the property's *current* income. If the tenant's lease term is about to expire and the tenant wants to stay, they will need to have their rental rate substantially increased. If the tenant opts not to renew their lease agreement, another tenant would quickly rent the property at a rental rate of $40,000-$45,000/year, providing you with higher rental income, while increasing the property's value.

If the tenant's current rental rate is level with market rental rates, then the length of the tenant's lease term becomes really important. The longer the lease term, the better.

An above market rental rate may seem like a good thing, but there needs to be caution exercised. What's going on? Did the area rental rates decline? If so, what was the cause? Was the tenant's prior rental history not as strong as it should be, so the rental rate had to be increased to offset the risk? There should be an explanation here. Sometimes, the landlord was just savvy. Other times, there's something going on that you should be aware of.

Chapter Six

APARTMENTS

Call property management companies for apartment buildings surrounding the subject property and inquire about their rental rates. The rental rates quoted must be from comparable apartment units (similar in age, location, amenities, and number of bedrooms) to the property you are looking to purchase. Alternatively, there may also be enough listings on Loopnet to see what similar apartments in the same area are renting for.

How Are Rental Rates Calculated?

RETAIL

Retail and office space is rented on a per square foot basis. Generally, smaller rental spaces command a higher per square foot rental rate, than much larger rental spaces do. For instance, you would not find the rental rate of a 500 Sq Ft office space to be the same as the rental rate of a 50,000 Sq Ft office space. That is why it is important, when comparing properties, that the rental space size is similar.

OFFICE

In addition to comparing the size of the rental space, the class of the property will determine the amount of rent that is reasonable. Office building space is usually classified as Class A, Class B, or Class C. There is no set standard for how office buildings are classified into each category. It is completely subjective. However, the four main factors usually considered are:

1. The property's age
2. The property's location
3. The property's amenities
4. The status of the property's tenants

The building's classification is always referenced from the point of a Class A building.

Class A

Describes the highest quality of office space available. It usually refers to a newer property that utilizes the highest quality of materials, attracts the highest quality of tenants, has the best location, and features the best amenities. This type of property works well for those businesses that need to provide a high-end perception to their clients, such as attorneys, banks, or investment companies.

Class B

While the location, materials, amenities, and tenants of these properties are good, they are not excellent, like the quality of a Class A building. There is little or no deferred maintenance or neglect of the property. These properties command less in rent than a Class A building.

Class C

These are usually older buildings that maintain a stable tenant base, but not of the upscale nature. They are functional, but are not overly esthetic. These properties are more affordable than Class A or Class B

81

buildings and work well for those businesses that need a location to conduct business, but don't need to impress their clients. A Class C building is usually attractive only for it's lower end rental rates.

If you purchase a Class C building, don't think you can raise the tenant's rental rates to those comparable of a Class A building. You would be sadly disappointed.

APARTMENTS

While retail and office spaces are rented on a per square foot basis, apartment rental rates are based upon the number of bedrooms within the apartment unit. You won't be able to command a much higher rental rate for a 1,100 Sq Ft, 2 bedroom apartment, than you can for a 800 Sq Ft, 2 bedroom apartment. It just doesn't work that way.

When comparing rental rates, the property's location and amenities are a large factor as well. That's why it's important when analyzing the rental rates of apartments for the comparable properties to be located close to the subject property and that both properties offer similar amenities. For instance, if you were comparing two bedroom units, one renting for $700/month and the other renting for $750/month, you may think, "Great, I can raise rents." However, it may be that the apartment renting for $750/month comes with an attached garage and has a community pool, while the other apartment doesn't come with those amenities.

Certain Types Of Tenants Are Riskier Than Others

RETAIL

Not all tenants are created equal. Certain types of businesses are more prone to dissolving than others. Think about the companies that manufactured typewriters or records. It's just a fact that as technology changes, some businesses will cease to exist when their product or service becomes obsolete.

One type of business that may soon become extinct due to technological advances, is the video rental store business. With all of the digital delivery technology available, how will their sales do in five, ten, or fifteen years, when you will probably be able to download any television program or movie from the comfort of your own home?

Technology isn't the only reason that a company may be forced to close it's doors. Another factor which may cause the sudden loss of a tenant is the down sizing or termination of an entire industry. That situation happened in San Francisco with the dot com crash. Within a very short period of time, a ton of office space became available for rent, causing the market rental rates to plunge from $70/Sq Ft to $20/Sq Ft.

The type of service or product your tenant offers their clients is just another factor to consider when analyzing a property. You want to purchase a property with your eyes open for all possible risks.

APARTMENTS

Are some of the tenants on Section 8? I think these tenants unjustly have a bad reputation. For some reason, many landlords think the people on this program are of poor caliber and will trash the property.

This simply is not true. Frankly, I wish all of my tenants were on Section 8. It takes a long time for people to get on this program. Most tenants don't want to risk losing their Section 8 voucher by being evicted. If a tenant does end up leaving his unit trashed, all you have to do is obtain a court judgement, and you will be paid back by HUD. In my opinion there is very little risk associated with renting to tenants on Section 8 and I'm all about less risk.

Here's some of the great benefits that come with renting to tenants on this program:

• Guaranteed payment sent directly to you from the government.
• Market rental rates are allowed.
• One or two year lease agreements are signed with the tenant.
• The program's paperwork is very easy.
• Less tenant turnover for you.
• If the tenant doesn't comply with the terms of their lease agreement, they may be removed from the program.

How Long Has The Tenant Been There?

RETAIL

Business owners spend a vast amount of money to build out their rental space to meet their business needs. Moving their company to another location would prove difficult, as their clients are accustomed to that particular location. They would need to change such things as their business cards, letter head, and telephone number, to name a few. It would be a mess. That's not even accounting for the additional expenses of improving the new rental space, the loss of productivity during that time, and the expense of moving. The longer the business is located at a particular place, the more difficult it is for them to move. A long tenant history also indicates a good payment history.

APARTMENTS

Unlike retail and office tenants, who tend to stay at one location for long periods of time, apartment tenants move much more frequently. It's rare to have a tenant rent at the same property for more than ten years. A long term apartment tenant may be considered someone who has lived at the property for over two years.

People get a sentimental attachment to their home, whether it is a property they own or not. Look at the property's rent roll and lease agreements to see how many tenants are new and how many tenants have been there a long time. If you find there are many long term tenants, they probably have no desire to go anywhere. If many of the tenants are new, find out what's causing the large tenant turnover.

ANALYZING THE LEASE AGREEMENT

Who Pays The Expenses?

Which property expenses the landlord or tenant pays, depends upon whether the lease is a *gross lease* or a *net lease*.

With a gross lease, typically used with apartments, the tenant pays a set amount, while the landlord is responsible for paying all the operating costs of the building.

Typically found in the retail sector, a net lease encompasses any one of three subcategories of net leases. You will need to get clarification as to which exact type of net lease is on the property, as the difference between the three different types of net leases is staggering.

RETAIL

TRIPLE NET (NNN) LEASES

The most common type of net lease is the *triple net (NNN) lease.* Big box stores such as Office Depot, Walmart, and Walgreens utilize this particular type of lease agreement. It is also often found with most fast food restaurants. A NNN lease is a beautiful set up for the real estate investor. If you want headache free, property ownership, this is the way for you to go.

There are many benefits of purchasing a property occupied with a NNN lease tenant. Let's discuss those benefits in detail.

BENEFITS OF A NNN LEASE

1. Most NNN Leases Are Corporate Guaranteed

If the tenant is a franchisee of a major corporation, the corporation will usually financially guarantee the tenant's lease agreement. This is a HUGE benefit for the landlord. For instance, if the tenant signed a 20 year lease agreement, but went out of business after five years, guess what? You would still have rental income from the property because it's corporation would fulfill the tenant's obligations under the lease agreement. The corporation could then sublease the property (if allowed in the lease agreement), leave the property vacant, or you could find a new tenant and offer the corporation a buy out option.

For instance, if a tenant was paying $240,000/year, with 15 years remaining on the lease term, by the end of the lease term, they would have paid $3,600,000, plus a huge sum of money for the property's other expenses such as property taxes, insurance, landscaping, utilities, etc. If you are able to find a different tenant who wants to lease the property, with terms that are acceptable to you, then you could offer the corporation the option of a lease buy out for $2,000,000 (I'm just throwing a figure out there!). I have never done this, but it seems like it would be a mutually beneficial deal.

Corporations are given a rating by Standard & Poor that evaluates their credit worthiness. If your tenant's lease is guaranteed by a strongly rated corporation, the property's future income can be considered money in the bank. However, if the tenant's lease agreement is guaranteed by a corporation that has a low Standard & Poor rating, who knows how beneficial that guarantee would prove to be.

2. The Tenant Pays All The Costs Of The Property

The benefit of this type of lease, is that the tenants are responsible for paying for the property's upkeep as if they owned it. They pay ALL of the property's expenses, including the property management fee. The rental amount paid to the landlord will have to pay the debt service (mortgage) on the property, but that is it.

Chapter Six

I really want to dive into how beneficial a NNN lease can be for a commercial real estate investor. Let's say you decide to purchase a commercial property for $5,000,000. You call the tax assessor's office and find out that the seller had purchased the property five years ago for $3,000,000. The current property tax amount is based upon the seller's $3,000,000 purchase price. However, if you purchase the property for $5,000,000, the tax assessor will use the new purchase price as the assessed value of the property. If the property tax rate is $2 per every $100 of the property's assessed value, then the yearly property tax due would increase from $60,000/year to $100,000/year. Guess what? You don't have to worry about it because the tenant is going to pay it, not you.

This is not the case with apartment buildings. When analyzing potential commercial properties to purchase remember that fact. The difference of who pays the property taxes can drastically impact your rate of return. The same goes for the property's other expenses such as utilities as well. Every year utility rates go up. Unless you have it negotiated in the lease agreement that the tenant pays his own utilities, you will have to come in with the extra money. Hopefully, you could raise the rental rates enough to cover the increased utility cost. If not, the money comes straight out of your pocketbook, not the tenant's pocketbook. With a NNN leased property, increased property expenses are not your problem.

3. Headache Free Property Ownership

Just sit back and collect your check.

4. The Lease May Contain A Percentage Rent Clause

An interesting provision that you will often find in a NNN

lease agreement with retail properties, that you will never find associated with residential properties, is a percentage rent clause. A *percentage rent clause* is a provision in the lease agreement that gives a "bonus" or additional rent to the landlord, based on the gross sales from the tenant's business. There is usually a "breakpoint" that must be hit before this clause is triggered.

A percentage rent clause is a pretty standard provision with tenants who are franchisees of companies such as Walgreens, Walmart, Rite Aid, or Albertsons, where the landlord will be given a certain percentage of the regular sales and a different percentage of the pharmaceutical sales. This clause can take an okay deal and make it great! We all know how expensive those drugs are!

If a percentage rent clause is not specifically mentioned in the property's offering package, ask the listing agent if there is one. When a commercial real estate agent lists a property, he sometimes neglects to put the fact that there is a percentage rent clause in the property's offering package. Other times, a commercial real estate agent may assume that all real estate investors know about it, which isn't the case.

A listing agent may try using the percentage rent clause as justification for a property's high asking price. I can see their point in doing this, as they are trying to get the best price for their client. However, there's usually a breakpoint that must be achieved before you will see any extra money. If that breakpoint is not hit, you will not receive any additional rent above and beyond the established base rent. Increasing a commercial property's asking price, due to the percentage rent clause, is like listing a home for sale at a price you think it will be worth two years down the road. Gotta give the real estate agent points for trying though!

5. The Tenant Takes Good Care Of The Property

The tenant knows that the property needs to be kept in good condition as their financial livelihood depends upon it. They will not delay fixing things like the roof because their inventory may be destroyed. They know they will pay for the repair now or later. It is so nice to know that your property will be maintained with a high standard of care, not only now, but for years to come.

THE NEGATIVE ASPECT OF NNN LEASES

1. The Rate Of Return Can Be Lower Than Other Types Of Commercial Real Estate Investments

Corporate guaranteed NNN leased properties are considered an extremely safe investment, so the investment rate of return will typically be lower than you could find with other commercial real estate investments. That increased rate of return on other types of commercial real estate investments must be countered with the risk of paying more expenses on your end. Especially, if you are looking to purchase apartments. If there is an increase in the cost of

> Increasing a commercial property's asking price due to the percentage rent clause, is like listing a home for sale at a price you think it will be worth two years down the road. Gotta give the real estate agent points for trying though!

garbage collection, property taxes, landscaping, or any other expense, it will come straight out of your wallet. Make sure you are comparing the rate of return on your money, factoring in all of the facts.

2. Fixed Rental Rate Increases

Most the time the tenant's rental rate increases will be established at the beginning of the lease term. If the market rental rates increase faster than what has been agreed upon when the lease was executed, then you may lose out on a higher rental rate in the future.

Double Net Lease (NN)

A *double net (NN) lease* is almost the same as a NNN lease, except that the landlord is responsible for the property's roof and building structure, and he may also be responsible to pay for the property's HVAC system and parking lot. While a NN lease may not seem that different from a NNN lease, the cost factor can be substantial. All of the items that the landlord is responsible to pay costs big bucks to repair or replace.

Net Lease

With a *net lease*, the tenant pays the rental amount, utilities, real estate taxes, and other special assessments that may be levied against the property. It's rare for retail tenants to be responsible for just these few items. At a minimum, a retail tenant will sign a NN lease.

Common Area Maintenance (CAM) Fees

If a commercial property contains many different businesses, then the tenants usually share the cost of maintaining the property's common areas. These shared expenses are called *Common Area Maintenance (CAM) Fees.* CAM fees are usually charged on a square foot basis, in addition to the tenant's rental rate.

For instance, if a tenant pays $10/Sq Ft to rent a 2,000 Sq Ft space, then their annual rent would be $20,000. However, if the lease agreement states the tenant's CAM fees are $1/Sq Ft, then the tenant would pay an additional $2,000/year, for a total rental amount of $22,000.

APARTMENTS

Because apartment tenants usually sign a gross lease, there's a lot more fluctuation to which expenses the landlord pays. The property expenses the landlord typically pays are property taxes, insurance, repairs, maintenance, improvements, landscaping, water, gas, garbage, and property management. The real variation in what a landlord pays is with utility expenses. The more utility costs you can pass on to the tenants, the better.

How Long Is The Lease Term?

RETAIL

A 30 year or longer lease term is not unheard of for tenants with a NNN lease. However, for smaller offices and retail stores, the lease term can range anywhere from one to 30 years. Many times there will be an initial lease term with right of renewal options. A *right of renewal* is a provision in the lease agreement which allows the tenant to renew the lease with specific terms under certain conditions.

The difference between the initial lease term and the right of renewal option is important in two main areas:

1. When Obtaining Financing With A Conventional Commercial Real Estate Lender

A right of renewal is a favorable provision for the tenant. However most people, including commercial real estate lenders, think it's a provision that's favorable for the landlord.

For instance, if a property has a 15 year lease term, with three, five year right of renewal options, then the lender will think, "Oh, good, the tenant has a 30 year lease term." when really they do not.

2. When Negotiating A Lease Agreement With A New Tenant Utilizing The Services Of A Leasing Agent

Another area where this is significant factor is when utilizing a leasing agent to negotiate a new lease agreement with a tenant. The leasing agent's commission will be based off of the initial lease term only. From a leasing commission point of view, you would be better off going with a shorter initial lease term with several right of renewal options, than you would be for one long lease term with no right of renewal options.

APARTMENTS

A one year lease term is standard with apartment tenants. After that time, a new lease agreement can be signed or the lease can automatically convert to a month to month agreement. While you will not get the benefits of a 30 year lease term like retail properties, a one year lease can be viewed in a positive light. Rental rates of apartments tend to increase faster than other types of commercial real estate do. If apartment tenants signed a lease with a long term, then you would not be able to increase their rental rate as often.

Rental Rate Increases

RETAIL/OFFICE

Rental rate increases are usually included in the terms of the lease agreement. The benefit of a long term lease agreement is the prospect of long term rental income. You can accurately project the property's cash flow far into the future. On the other end, if the market rental rate increase at a faster pace than what is agreed upon in the lease agreement, you will not be able to take advantage of that fact. There are provisions that can be written into the lease agreement that can compensate for this though.

APARTMENTS

Rental rate increases for apartments can occur when the initial lease term has expired. Constant awareness of comparable market rental rates will determine if the rental rate should be maintained at it's current rate or increased at that time.

How Large Is The Tenant's Security Deposit?

We all want tenants to pay a BIG security deposit. In addition to providing you security against future losses, security deposits are credited to the buyer at closing, which can be used to decrease closing costs. Each state has it's own laws that dictate how the tenant's security deposits must be handled. You will need to research those laws to make sure you comply with them.

Who Manages The Property?

Are you going to be obligated to continue using the existing property management company in place? Generally, you are not. However, this may hold true in the retail sector. You will want to make sure you investigate the property's current management company. You will be working closely with these people, so you must be on the same page on how the property should be managed. Remember, that the property management company works for you. They should manage the property around your preferences. We will discuss property management in depth in Chapter 13.

Who Pays For Improvements?

RETAIL

Most of the time, a retail tenant's rental space is rented as a shell. Can you imagine trying to rent an apartment that way?

"Oh, you would like carpet? You better go buy some! You need cabinets? I know of a great place that may give you a discount."

It just doesn't work that way. It's rare for a tenant in an apartment complex to spend their own money to improve your property. But, it's a standard scenario for tenants of retail properties.

When you own a new or vacant retail building, the tenant improvements will be negotiated before the initial lease agreement is ever signed. But what happens five years down the road, when the tenant wants to make a change to the property?

Tenants are usually not permitted to do any major changes to the property without the landlord's express, written consent. If the improvement is something that may prove beneficial to another tenant, you may grant the tenant permission to go ahead with the improvement. Once that tenant vacates the premises, the improvement remains. However, if the improvement that the tenant requests would not be helpful in releasing the property, you may grant permission to the tenant only if they agree to bring the property back to it's original condition when they vacate the property.

Tenant Improvement Allowances

Many times, especially with new construction, tenants are given credits, called *tenant improvement allowances,* that offsets the tenant's rental rate for a certain period of time. This financially helps the tenant build out their rental space to meet their business needs.

You shouldn't waste your time or money trying to anticipate what improvements a potential tenant will want. The tenant will build out the property to their own specifications. Think about it. If your vacant property used to be leased by Burger King, and now McDonalds wants to lease the property, the McDonald's corporation will have specific requirements as to which type of improvements the building is required to have. They will dictate such things as what kind of walls, fixtures and tiles must be used. Any improvement you did would just be removed anyway.

EXISTING FINANCING

Can you imagine the following scenario when purchasing a residential investment property?

"Hello, Mr. Seller. My name is Monica. I really love your house and would like to buy it. I'll just assume the existing mortgage. How does that sound?"

It's a difficult scenario to believe because you won't find many sellers who would agree to it and most residential real estate loans are not assumable. However, this scenario happens all the time in commercial real estate deals.

Many commercial real estate loans are assumable. In fact, the seller may REQUIRE that the buyer assumes the existing mortgage because it has a substantial prepayment penalty or a lock out. Assumable mortgages often have a loan assumption fee of 1-2% of the loan balance which you should request the seller to pay.

> Many commercial real estate loans are assumable. In fact, the seller may REQUIRE that the buyer assumes the existing mortgage because it has a substantial prepayment penalty or a lock out.

We will go into financing in detail in Chapter 10. At this point what you need to know is whether or not there is an existing assumable mortgage on the property. If the existing mortgage is assumable, then it can be a pivotal factor in your decision of whether you decide to purchase the property or not.

For instance, if the market interest rate for a commercial loan is 10%, but the subject property has an existing assumable mortgage with a below market interest rate of 8%, the subject property is a much better value than a commercial property without an assumable mortgage.

WHICH TYPE OF OWNERSHIP INTEREST ARE YOU BUYING?

FREEHOLD OR LEASEHOLD?

Most of the time when a commercial property is for sale, it includes the land and building. You would be buying a *freehold* or a "fee simple" ownership interest in the property. Other times, the building and land are owned and sold separately. In that case, you would be purchasing a freehold interest in the building combined with a *leasehold* ownership interest in the land.

Leasehold interests are extremely common in certain areas, such as Hawaii. With a leasehold interest, the ownership of the building may revert back to the land owner after the lease term expires.

I personally don't like leasehold arrangements. To emphasize how purchasing a leasehold interest can be a negative situation, I'll tell you about a property listing I saw. The property was a hotel with a $1,300,000 list price which initially seemed to be a great price-until I found out the building was on a ground lease. In this particular case, you would be purchasing the business, the building, and a leasehold interest in the land.

The ground lease payments for the previous year were $96,000, plus a percentage of the business revenue (percentage rent clause). The previous year, at only a 52% occupancy level, that percentage rent came out to an additional $30,000 above the $96,000 base rent. So, what would happen if you were able to really ramp up the business?

I can guarantee you'd be paying at least an additional $20,000. You would need to be prepared to pay a total rental amount of $146,000 ($96,000 base rent + $50,000 percentage rent of the increased business revenue). You would probably be able to purchase another $1,500,000 worth of real estate for the same payment.

So, what's the true price of the property? It's comparable to purchasing a property priced at $2,800,000 ($1,300,000 list price plus $1,500,000 value of the ground lease).

But the real problem was the fact that there was only 14 years left on the ground lease. What would happen to the building after the ground lease term expired? Would the building revert back to the land owner, as is usually the case? You would have to negotiate a new longer term ground lease to even consider purchasing the property (which terms may be beneficial to you, but I doubt it). I do have to say that the land owner has done a very good job negotiating the terms of the ground lease.

Some people find a leasehold favorable because it allows the buyer to come in with less money. That is a valid point. I'm not saying that you should or shouldn't buy a building on a ground lease. I just want you to be aware of the benefits, and the downfalls, of doing so. I would rather fix my land cost by purchasing the building and the land together. That way, I would be making a fixed payment to the bank, while receiving the benefit of the land's appreciation, without sharing a percentage of the business revenue.

WHAT EXACTLY ARE YOU BUYING?

How are you viewing the property you are thinking of buying? Are you looking at it as one element? Maybe all you see is the land and the building as one unit. However, you are not purchasing just one thing. Real estate has many different components. By being able to see real estate's different components, you may realize value in a commercial property, that other real estate investors flat miss.

Water (Riparian) Rights

Water rights, the right to capture and use water, is an asset that may be sold or leased. Here in Las Vegas, water is a precious commodity. Southern Nevada's water department is negotiating with farmers in Northern Nevada to pump water to us. Of course, they would be paid generously for that right.

Water rights may or may not, come with a property. There may be a property you are looking to purchase, where the property owner isn't even aware they own the water rights. Each state has it's own laws that must be complied with in order to claim water rights. Find out if water rights come with the property. If so, it can create an additional source of cash *flow*. Did you get it? Cash flow....Okay, so I'm not a comedian....Moving on!

Airspace Rights

I know it sounds strange, but air can be worth a lot of money. When you own land, you also own the air above it. The question is, "How high?" The answer depends upon the zoning of your property. If the zoning indicates that you would only be able to build up to 35 feet, then that is where your airspace rights end.

Let's say that the zoning for a 75 feet high building you are looking to purchase, allows a building height up to 100 feet. Located close to the building you want to purchase is a piece of land that a developer wants to build a 120 feet high building. If you bought the 75 feet high building and had no intention of increasing it's height, you may want to sell your extra 25 feet of airspace to the developer who needs it. This transaction would have to be approved by the local government officials as well. Many people, including Donald Trump, have paid big money for air.

Mineral Rights

A mineral right is the right to extract minerals from the earth or to receive a royalty for the extraction of minerals. Mineral rights includes oil, natural gas, coal, gold, copper, iron, limestone, gypsum, building stones, salt, gravel, and sand. You may buy, sell or lease these rights as the owner of the land. Mineral rights are sold or leased separately from the surface of the land.

Most of the time, you won't have much need for mineral rights. But what if you were looking to purchase a 500 acre mountain resort? You better make sure you have mineral rights. There very well could be valuable minerals in the land.

The royalties from mineral extraction could make you wealthy many times over.

Know what you are buying. Realize, and take advantage of the fact, that real estate encompasses more components than just the land and the building.

WHAT NOBODY TELLS YOU

1. The more you know about a property and it's tenants, the better decisions you can make.
2. When analyzing commercial real estate you must make sure you are comparing apples to apples.
3. A NNN lease is a headache free way to own commercial real estate.
4. A seller may require that you assume a commercial property's existing mortgage when you purchase the property.
5. There's more to real estate than just land and buildings.

IT'S ALL ABOUT THE NUMBERS

YOU THOUGHT YOU WERE DONE WITH MATH!

When you left school, you probably thought the need to do mathematical calculations was forever gone. I'm sorry to inform you, but when analyzing commercial real estate, you will need to know how to calculate a few very important formulas, to determine if the property's numbers posted by the seller or his listing agent, are accurate. It also allows you to come up with a precise value for the commercial property you are looking to purchase. Remember, in commercial real estate, the value of a property is all about the numbers.

How Commercial Real Estate Is Valued

A residential property's value is based upon neighboring property values or "comps." Lenders and potential buyers of residential properties will not take the residential property's additional rental income into consideration because that's not how residential properties are valued. For instance, if you owned a residential investment property that rented for $1,500/month, while all the other landlords in the neighborhood were only receiving $1,200/month in rent, that additional $300 monthly rental income you were receiving wouldn't make any difference to your property's value.

It's the completely opposite situation with commercial real estate. Very simply, the more money the property brings in, the more it's worth. What you are really purchasing when you buy commercial real estate, is the property's cash flow with the building thrown in as a bonus.

> I'm sure many uneducated real estate investors have been suckered into purchasing overpriced commercial real estate because they didn't understand that the numbers listed in the property's offering package, were not the actual numbers.

Proforma

A *proforma* is a outline of how a commercial property should financially perform in a make-believe, fantasy world. Many times, the seller or the listing agent, will use a proforma in the offering package and base the asking price off of the proforma, instead of using the property's "real" numbers.

There's usually one of two reasons why they do this. First, the listing agent is hoping that an ignorant investor comes along and over pays for the property. Or, second, the property's actual numbers are so bad, that if the listing agent used them, nobody would purchase the property.

I have to hand it to those sellers and real estate agents who try to get away with this. I'm sure many uneducated real estate investors have been suckered into purchasing overpriced commercial real estate because they didn't understand that the numbers listed in the property's offering package, were not the actual numbers. Unless the property is brand new, there's no reason to buy it for a price based off of proforma numbers. **Purchase a property for a price based upon it's actual numbers only!**

Let's all do an exercise right now. Put your right hand up and repeat after me. "I promise not to buy a commercial property based off of proforma numbers." I can't hear you. Let's say it again. "I promise not to buy a property based off of proforma numbers." Okay, I feel much better now. As silly as this may be, you can tell how I feel about this.

Then again, the actual numbers the seller lists, may not be the property's actual numbers either. You must be a detective in figuring out the property's actual numbers, to get the most accurate idea of what you are potentially buying. It is so easy for the seller to manipulate the property's numbers to paint a pretty picture that is not accurate of it's true financial performance.

GET OUT THOSE CALCULATORS

Let's get started with some definitions and calculations....

Gross Operating Income (GOI)

Gross operating income (GOI) is the total annual income derived from the property. It includes not only rental income, but any additional money generated from the property. There is a lot of money to be made from other sources such as laundry, vending, and late fees. Maybe you can find an uneducated seller who only calculates rental income into the gross operating income, enabling you to purchase the property for less than it's really worth.

Vacancy Allowance

The *vacancy allowance* is the expected or actual vacancy level for the property. Even if the property is 100% occupied, a standard vacancy level of 5-10% should be used. However, that doesn't mean that if the property has a 25% vacancy level, that only 10% should be used in your calculations. It simply means that you should be using either the actual vacancy level or a 5-10% minimum vacancy level. For instance, if a property generates $750,000 of annual rental income, but there is a 15% vacancy level, then you would calculate the vacancy allowance as follows:

$750,000 X .15 = $112,500 Vacancy Allowance

With this example, the $112,500 vacancy allowance would be subtracted from the property's GOI.

OPERATING EXPENSES

Operating expenses are the annual cumulative expenses that occur in the course of owning the property, such as property taxes, repairs, landscaping, maintenance, property management, utilities, and advertising. Basically, anytime you have to cut a check to keep the property operating, it is put into this category.

What Will It Take For YOU To Operate The Property?

You should calculate the operating expenses to reflect what it would take for YOU to run the property. While the seller's operating expenses provide a nice guideline, you can't use those numbers to come up with an accurate figure for what it would cost you to operate the property. You won't have to worry about calculating operating expenses when purchasing a property with a NNN lease tenant in place. For those types of commercial properties all you need to know is the property's Net Operating Income (NOI).

Which Expenses Are Not Operating Expenses?

Upon selling a commercial property, you will need to subtract the operating expenses of the property that are unique to you. For instance, you may have utilized the services of a bookkeeper or property manager, while the new buyer may choose not to. Mortgage payments are not considered an operating expense as well because it's an expense that the owner chooses to have. Someone can purchase the property with cash and that expense would not exist.

Let's look at some specific operating expenses in detail that you may be responsible for as a commercial real estate owner.

Property Taxes

Property taxes are a HUGE property expense. Knowing how much this expense will be is critical. The seller will indicate the property tax expense, but should you use that figure? No. Most counties will adjust the property's assessed value every time the property is sold based upon the purchase price. If your seller bought the property for $1,000,000 and was paying

1% annually or $10,000, when he sells the property to you for $2,000,000, then the tax assessor will use the $2,000,000 purchase price as the property's new assessed value. Instead of the property taxes being $10,000 annually, they would be $20,000 annually.

There may also be special tax assessments associated with the property that you are not aware of which you would be obligated to pay. To avoid any surprises call the county tax assessor's office where the property is located to find out what the tax rate for the property is. Don't know what to say? You can say something like this:

"Hi, my name is Monica. I may be purchasing the property located at 123 ABC St. I was wondering what the tax rate is for that property? If I decide to purchase the property, will the purchase price be the new assessed value? Are there any special assessments associated with the property that I should to be aware of? Is there any other information you could provide me with that you think I would find helpful?"

The seller will indicate the property tax expense, but should you use that figure? No. Most counties will adjust the property's assessed value every time the property is sold based upon the purchase price.

Can you see how this conversation with the tax assessor would be helpful? You are trying to minimize as many financial surprises as possible, that you will surely discover after you have closed on the property.

Property Management

Fulfilling the role as the property manager when you were investing in residential properties was fine. But now that you are in the real estate big leagues, that needs to change. You will need to hire either an individual or a company to handle the daily property management duties. If there is no dollar figure in the property's financials for this expense, find out what the going rate is to hire someone and put that figure in your budget. Property management is discussed in detail in Chapter 13.

Inspections

If you purchase apartments be aware that there may be annual inspection expenses. For instance you may have to have an annual inspection by the city to renew the building's Certificate of Occupancy. It can be quite a large expense. I just paid $1,765 for this expense for my Ohio property. Or, if the apartment complex has a community pool does it require an annual inspection to operate it?

This is the case with my condo conversion property in Redding, California. During the pool inspection, the inspector found that the stair railing didn't comply because it didn't extend beyond the third step. What I have yet to figure out, is how the pool passed inspection for over 30 years with a non compliant hand rail! The non complying hand rail cost $1,000 to have replaced-an expense I hadn't counted on.

Do you see how these inspections and the associated costs of repairing the deficiencies found can add up? If you don't have any money allotted in the financials for inspections and their associated expenses to repair the deficiencies, then your rate

109

of return may be lower than you anticipated.

Repairs

You will have repair expenses every month. It's just a fact. If your tenants don't submit repair requests every month, something is wrong (unless you are leasing to a tenant with a NNN lease). When evaluating the repair figure supplied by the seller, scrutinize it closely. Does the figure seem low? If so, it may mean there's a bunch of deferred maintenance. Also ask the seller if the resident manager performed the repairs. If so, a big warning light should be flashing in your mind. Most resident managers do not have the proper knowledge to repair items correctly.

Let me just say, that in the course of owning 81 apartment units, I've seen some really odd repairs. For instance, there was a lighting problem in one of the apartment units in Redding. When my contractor removed the light switch panel he discovered that someone had previously "repaired" the wiring using stereo wire. Obviously, that wire had to be removed and replaced with the correct type of wire.

Let me just say, that in the course of owning 81 apartment units, I've seen some really odd repairs. For instance, there was a lighting problem in one of the apartment units in Redding. When my contractor removed the light switch panel he discovered that someone had previously "repaired" the wiring using stereo wire.

If the repair figure seems high, try to figure out if it was because of something unusual. Did the seller's contractor over charge for his services? I've realized how substantially different the same repair can cost. In Ohio, I can get a three bedroom apartment painted, including materials for $400. In Redding, the property manager hired a painting contractor who charged over $2,000 to paint a two bedroom apartment. That is a major price difference for the same amount of work. Obviously, I was getting ripped off by the Redding painting contractor.

You see, a very high or very low repair figure is not necessarily a good or bad thing. It just should raise questions that need answered before proceeding with the property purchase. After owning a couple of commercial properties, you will acquire a feel for what repairs should cost. Until then, you may be taken advantage of.

Improvements (Capital Expenses)

While repairs can be regularly anticipated, future improvements cannot. It doesn't take much, like needing to replace a HVAC system to the tune of $4,000, to put a big dent in your pocketbook. Therefore, a certain amount of money should be allocated as a reserve for those future improvements. If you don't have some kind of reserve fund in place, you will be financially "up a creek."

I am personally bad, bad, bad, about doing this. I just can't justify having money sitting in the bank doing nothing for me. My financial cushion is having large enough credit card lines that can be accessed as needed to cover any large, unexpected expense.

Whichever way you plan to pay for improvements, you will need to count on the fact that there will be big expenses that will come your way during the course of owning commercial real estate. The good news is that many of the improvements will improve the energy efficiency of the property, which qualify for rebate programs and/or tax credits.

Utilities

We all know that the price of utilities doesn't go down. What you want to find out, is, who is responsible to pay for the water, sewer, electric, gas, and trash. Any utility expense that you can pass onto the tenant, is money in the bank for you. Reducing utility costs is an easy way of creating value in a commercial property. We will discuss more about increasing your property's value in Chapter 14. For now, be aware that you will need to verify who pays which utility expense. Then calculate the utility expense for what you, as the landlord are responsible, by taking the current utility costs and adding 10% to compensate for the ever increasing utility rates.

Property Insurance

Another area where owning residential real estate is different than owning commercial real estate is how previous insurance claims are tracked. With residential real estate, the insurance claim follows you, as an individual. With commercial real estate, the insurance claim stays with the property. So, if the commercial property you are looking to purchase has a prior insurance claim on it, irregardless of the fact that you didn't own it at the time the claim was filed, then you should expect to pay a higher than normal insurance rate.

If you plan on obtaining conventional commercial real estate financing, the lender may require you to come up with a full year of insurance premiums prior to closing. The lender may also dictate what the minimum deductible on the policy must be. I was unpleasantly surprised about this large up front expense on my first commercial real estate purchase. You can change the deductible and switch to monthly payments after closing.

Professional Fees

As the result of owning commercial real estate you will need to seek guidance from experienced professionals. You will need the help of an attorney to review purchase contracts and file evictions. You will need a CPA to prepare your business tax return. You will need a bookkeeper to input all of the property's income and expenses and ensure your books balance. You will need to anticipate how much money to set aside to pay the fees associated with this professional help.

Landscaping

You must hire someone, whether it is an individual or a company to maintain the property's landscaping. This includes picking up the trash that naturally comes onto the property. This can be a big budget item as well. Once, I tried to have my onsite managers be responsible for the landscaping. That was a mess. It just was too much for them to take on with their other responsibilities. So, I hired my mom instead. I knew she would get the job done right.

Whoever you decide to hire, make sure someone is doing it consistently. If the outside of your commercial property looks like a dump, then the prospective tenants will think the inside is a dump too.

Chapter Seven

Amenities

When you purchase a house that you will personally live in, you will look at that property with a different set of eyes than you will when purchasing an investment property. For instance, most people would love to have a swimming pool at their home. However, as a commercial real estate investor, a pool may be looked at as an additional expense and a potential liability problem.

Any amenity, like a pool or a workout room, will have associated maintenance and repair costs. The associated costs of providing those amenities for the tenants has to be weighed against the financial benefit of charging higher rental rates.

Miscellaneous Expenses

There may be additional miscellaneous expenses that have to be paid, such as travel to the property, annual corporate renewal fees, bank fees, and advertising. Small expenses start adding up and will need to be calculated into the property's financials as well.

Net Operating Income (NOI)

PAY VERY CLOSE ATTENTION HERE! The property's *Net Operating Income (NOI)* is considered the "gold standard" in determining the value of commercial real estate. The NOI is calculated by taking the property's GOI and subtracting the vacancy allowance and the operating expenses. The figure remaining is the NOI.

Let's do an example. Let's say that a property you are looking to purchase has a GOI of $150,000. The vacancy allowance is

$15,000 and the operating expenses are $50,000. This is how the calculation would look:

GOI	$150,000
Vacancy Allowance	$15,000
Operating Expenses	$50,000
NOI	**$85,000**

Mortgage payments are not calculated as an operating expense. **Any mortgage payment that you make will have to be paid out of the NOI. Therefore, the NOI must be higher than the property's annual mortgage payments or the property will have a negative cash flow!**

To derive the value of the property you should divide the NOI by the customary cap rate (we will discuss cap rate in just a minute) for the area where the property is located. For instance, using the example above, the property's NOI is $85,000. If the cap rate is 10% then you would come up with a property value of $850,000 calculated as follows:

$$\frac{\$85,000 \text{ NOI}}{10\% \text{ Cap Rate}} = \$850,000 \text{ Property Value}$$

After we explore what a cap rate is, you will be able to recalculate the numbers to offer the seller a purchase price that will allow your personal criteria to be met.

Cash On Cash Return

The *cash on cash return* is my personal gold standard that I use when analyzing the potential of a commercial property I plan to hold long term. The cash on cash return is the rate of return you receive on the money you personally put into the deal. For instance, if you made an annual net profit of $25,000 (after mortgage payments) on a commercial property that you put a $100,000 down payment on, you would have made a 25% cash on cash return.

$25,000 Annual Net Income (Includes mortgage) = 25% Cash On Cash
$100,000 Money Invested   Return

The cash on cash return is important because it takes into account much more than just the NOI. It factors into the equation how much money you personally have invested into the property. The less of your own personal money you put into the deal, the higher your cash on cash return would be.

To highlight the significance of this, let's recalculate the cash on cash return of the same example above except this time let's say the seller agreed to hold a $50,000, 8% interest only, second mortgage. Instead of coming into the deal with $100,000, you would only need to come in with $50,000. The new cash on cash return, utilizing the second mortgage scenario, would be calculated as follows:

$25,000 Previous Annual Net Profit
-$4,000 Yearly Second Mortgage Payment
$21,000 Annual Net Income

$21,000 Annual Net Income = 42% Cash On Cash
$50,000 Money Invested   Return

This calculation gives you an insight as to how to take a good return, and make it into a fantastic one, by finding ways to come into the deal with less of your own money.

Gross Rent Multiplier (GRM)

The *Gross Rent Mulitiplier* (GRM) is an equation some real estate investors use to express the value of a property calculated by using the property's annual income and it's "market value." The GRM fails to provide enough information by itself to analyze whether one commercial property is a better value than another commercial property because the property's expenses are not factored into the equation. In fact, I find this equation so useless, I don't even know why I'm putting it in here. Well, actually the reason is so when you eventually sell your commercial property, and someone asks you what the property's GRM is, you will have the answer. Beyond that it's an equation that really is of no value.

The GRM is calculated by taking the property's market value and diving it by the property's annual rental income. For example, if the market value of a property is $1,500,000, and the property's annual rental income is $200,000, then the GRM is calculated as follows:

$1,500,000 Market Value Of The Property = 7.5 GRM
$200,000 Property's Annual Rental Income

If you are looking to purchase an apartment building that has a 7.5 GRM, but find the surrounding apartment buildings have a 10 GRM, then you *may* have found yourself a bargain. Further financial information would be necessary to find out for sure.

Chapter Seven

Capitalization Rate (Cap rate)

The *capitalization rate* or "cap rate" is another important definition, so pay attention, my dear students. The cap rate is calculated by dividing the property's NOI by the purchase price of the property. For instance, if you bought a property for $1,000,000, and it's NOI was $100,000, then the cap rate calculation would look like this:

$$\frac{\$100,000 \text{ NOI}}{\$1,000,000 \text{ Purchase Price}} = 10\% \text{ Cap Rate}$$

From an income point of view, the higher the cap rate, the better. I generally look for a cap rate of 10 to 13 % for properties I plan to hold long term.

Many commercial real estate investors and commercial lenders view those commercial properties with a higher than average cap rate as riskier properties. I don't understand how this perception came to be. When making true comparisons, it just doesn't make sense. How can a A+ corporate guaranteed, NNN leased property with a 10% cap rate, be riskier than a A+ corporate guaranteed, NNN leased property with a 8% cap rate? Just because you found a property that has a higher than average cap rate does not mean there is something wrong or risky with the property. After looking at many commercial properties on Loopnet, you will find that the property's cap rate will not always reflect the risk of the property.

CAN'T GET ENOUGH?

If you're just itching to learn more about analyzing commercial real estate cash flow you should read, *What Every Real Estate Investor Needs To Know About Cash Flow...And 36 Other Key Financial Measures*, by Frank Gallinelli. Seriously, it is the best book I've ever read about how to evaluate and calculate the numbers of commercial real estate. Frank Gallinelli has also developed a software program that calculates these numbers for you. Printing the property's cash flow report could be a key feature of any loan package that you will submit to a commercial lender as well. You can't dispute the numbers when they are staring you right in the face.

WHAT NOBODY TELLS YOU

1. In commercial real estate, the property's value is all about it's income.
2. Inspect the property's reported income and expenses with a fine tooth comb to get an accurate picture of what you are buying.
3. Don't use proforma numbers to come up with a property's value.
4. NOI is the gold standard used when calculating the value of commercial real estate.
5. Evaluate what it would cost for YOU to operate the property, not what it cost the seller to operate the property.

CHAPTER 8
LOCK THE PROPERTY UP

Y ou have spent a great amount of time learning how to analyze commercial real estate and want to proceed to the next step. What is that next step? You must LOCK THE PROPERTY UP. In English, I mean write up a purchase offer. If you find a fantastic property, don't hesitate to act quickly. While there is far less competition in the commercial real estate investing world, than there is in the residential real estate investing world, the properties with the highest financial potential are put under contract very quickly. You are competing against major league real estate investment players, who can recognize fantastic investment properties as quickly as you do.

Lock It Up First

Many real estate investors will want to view the property first, then submit an offer to purchase it. That is all backwards! Viewing the property first may work if you are investing in residential properties located within your own city. But what's the point of looking at a property if you and the seller can't agree upon the purchase price? You'd be wasting a lot of time and money. Locking the property up with a purchase contract does not obligate you to buy the property. It only obligates the seller to sell it to you. You will use the "due diligence" time frame to evaluate whether or not you will proceed with the purchase of the property.

You Won't Close On All Of The Properties You Put Under Contract

You will not close every property that you put under contract. In fact, I would worry if you did. My closing rate is around 50% of the commercial properties that I put under contract. My first commercial property I put under contract looked great on paper. However, based upon the results of the inspection, I decided not to move forward with the purchase. I closed on the next property, the one after that, but not the fourth one.

> **Locking the property up with a purchase contract does not obligate you to buy the property. It only obligates the seller to sell it to you.**

COMMERCIAL REAL ESTATE AGENTS

During the course of investing in commercial real estate you will have a lot of interaction with commercial real estate agents. Your knowledge of what to expect from them will help you out tremendously.

I'm going to apologize right now to all of the real estate agents out there who are reading this book because what I'm going to discuss next will probably piss you off. But, these things must be in this book, as they are important for novice commercial real estate investors to know. We will discuss such things as:

● **The common "tricks of the trade" real estate agents utilize when selling commercial real estate.**

They will not like having their secrets revealed.

● **The fact that they don't always know what they are doing**.

Most commercial real estate agents don't own commercial real estate themselves. It's like me, as a dental hygienist, spending my days preaching of the benefits of flossing, yet failing to floss my own teeth. Yet, this is the case with most real estate agents. They spend their day preaching about the benefits of investing in real estate, when they personally don't take advantage of those benefits. I have a hard time fathoming this.

● **They lack creativity when "marketing" a listing.**

Another frustration I have with real estate agents is the lack of creativity they display when listing a client's property. I don't call placing a listing on the MLS or on Loopnet, then waiting for other real estate agents to submit purchase offers, "marketing." There should be more effort made than that when selling a property.

It's not that real estate agents aren't good people. Some of my best friends are real estate agents. I just need you to be aware of what goes on in the commercial real estate investing world, so you will be prepared to handle situations with specific knowledge in mind. Knowing what to expect when working with real estate agents is a part of that.

Use The Right Type Of Real Estate Agent

You will find out quickly that commercial real estate transactions are complex. As I've said before, it's a whole different ball game. When you are just learning the ropes of commercial real estate investing, you will need some help.

You want to work with real estate agents who have more experience than you do, so they can guide you through the process. You generally will not find someone with that level of experience needed for these types of deals if they are a residential real estate agent. For instance, if you asked a residential real estate agent what a cap rate is, they probably wouldn't be able to give you the answer. How can they help you, if they don't know the rules of the commercial real estate investing game either?

Commercial real estate agents are better equipped to help novice commercial real estate investors navigate through the complexities of a commercial real estate transaction. There's no reason to have a "run of the mill" residential real estate agent representing you with the purchase of a large retail development. It's way out of their league.

An exception to this may be if you are looking to purchase apartment buildings. Two of the real estate agents I have used on previous commercial real estate transactions are both former general contractors. They brought a ton of experience about building and construction to the table that other residential real estate agents don't have. Although they are residential real estate agents, as all of my commercial properties I have bought have been apartment buildings, their particular knowledge was extremely valuable to me.

Just as with any other profession, you will find all kinds of commercial real estate agents. Who you choose to work with can make a significant difference in the experiences you have when investing in commercial real estate. Choose your real estate agent wisely.

Be Represented By Your Own Agent

Unless, the seller has no listing agent, I prefer to be represented by my own real estate agent, rather than doing a deal without one. It's not like the seller's real estate agent is going to rebate to you half of the commission he would have otherwise split with another real estate agent. Plus, my negotiation skills are weak. I need someone who can do that on my behalf.

Find A Local Real Estate Agent

Real estate agents are regulated and licensed by the state in which they conduct business. If you live in Nevada, and want to purchase a property in California, then you would need a California licensed real estate agent to submit the purchase offer. This is good practice anyway because every state has different laws and regulations that only a local agent would know. They know the area better, so they will know such things as:

Who typically pays the closing costs?
How quickly does real estate sell in the area?
Special circumstances unique to that particular area.

If the property you want to purchase is located out of state, ask real estate agents in your area for a recommendation for a real estate agent in the area where the property is located.

After asking around, you should contact the recommended real estate agents by telephone to see if any of them will work out for you.

Make Sure Your Personalities Match

Since you will be working closely with your real estate agent, find someone who will compliment your personality. If you are assertive, then you may want to work with someone who is assertive too, to match your personality. For instance, with my assertive personality, I find it annoying to work with someone who's overly diplomatic or consistently worries about offending people.

On the other hand, if you are a diplomatic type, an assertive real estate agent may rub you the wrong way. Sometimes, it is nice to work with someone who has the opposite personality you do as a balance, like a yin/yang type of situation. Decide ahead of time, what personality type you wish your real estate agent to have, so you can quickly find one who fits that requirement.

Make Contact With The Listing Agent

You will have already contacted the seller's listing agent during your analysis phase. That initial point of contact probably gave you insight into the type of person you will be dealing with on the deal.

Make sure you clarify with the listing agent, on your very first telephone conversation, that you are represented by your own real estate agent. Explain how you look at so many properties that you don't involve your real estate agent until you are ready to write up an offer. The reason this is necessary is because listing agents get all excited when they get a call from a "principal." A *principal* is a buyer who is not represented by another real estate agent. The listing agent gets excited because he is already seeing the extra dollar signs in his mind from not having to split his commission with another real estate agent.

Here's how I learned that lesson. I once found a property located in Columbus, Ohio, that I thought might be worth placing a telephone call to the listing agent about. After speaking to the listing agent, I was interested in pursuing the property further. I called my Ohio real estate agent, Marvin, to let him know I was interested in writing an offer on the property. Marvin then proceeded to call the listing agent to ask him a few more questions for which he needed clarification. Well, the listing agent got all in a frenzy because he thought I misrepresented myself. He simply assumed, because I had personally called, that I didn't have my own real estate agent.

I never like to leave issues unresolved, so I emailed the listing agent to explain to him that as a full time real estate investor, I look at so many properties, I only involve my real estate agent when I'm ready to write up an offer. The fact that my real estate agent was calling him, was a good sign.

COMMON PLOYS REAL ESTATE AGENTS AND SELLERS USE WHEN SELLING COMMERCIAL REAL ESTATE

Commercial real estate agents are sales people. They usually do not own commercial real estate themselves. They will not know any more than you do, as to what constitutes a "good" investment property. Their goal is to sell the properties they have listed for the highest price possible, in order to achieve the highest commission. Sometimes they have to get creative in order to accomplish this goal. It is of the utmost importance that you recognize the common ploys that real estate agents and sellers use when selling commercial real estate.

They Create A Sense Of Urgency

I can almost guarantee that every time you speak with a real estate agent about a commercial property, he will say something like this;"You better hurry. There's been a lot of interest on this property. It won't last long." Interest doesn't mean anything. A Letter of Intent (LOI) doesn't mean anything. Only a signed purchase contract means something, but even then, not a whole lot. It's all a game. Even if there has legitimately been a lot of interest on the property and you miss out on this one particular deal, there's another one just down the road. There are literally thousands of commercial properties for sale from which to choose.

Even when the property goes into contract, it doesn't mean the story is over. When I bought the condo conversion property, it had gone into contract three previous times. In fact, I don't think the seller truly thought we were going to close on the deal because he had been disappointed three times before. Even if the property is in contract you may want to give the listing agent your contact information just in case the property doesn't close. When that happens (and it will), you will be in a great position to purchase the property at a much better price than you could have before. The seller's desire to have the property sold will be much stronger at that point, resulting in greater flexibility with the property's selling price and/or terms.

They Post A Proforma Instead Of Using The Property's "Real" Numbers

We just discussed this in the last chapter. There's usually a reason why real estate agents do this. Either the "real" numbers are so bad that the asking price is way out of line, or the real estate agent is hoping that an ignorant real estate investor will pay more than the property is worth. The only time proforma numbers should be used to set the asking price for a property, is when the property is brand new. In that case, there would be no way for the actual numbers to be used because there are none.

They Manipulate The Numbers To Make The Property Look Like It Generates More Money Than It Does

> **Trim a few expenses off here and there; Make the numbers believable of course. With just a few quick changes, the property is magically worth hundreds of thousands of dollars more.**

I really can't blame the seller for doing this. I know that when the time comes to sell my commercial properties, I might suddenly develop Alzheimer's regarding some of the property's expenses. Trim a few expenses off here and there; Make the numbers believable, of course. With just a few quick changes, the property is magically worth hundreds of thousands of dollars more. *DON'T EVER TRUST THE SELLER'S NUMBERS TO BE ACCURATE.*

129

Chapter Eight

They Do The Math Wrong

Unfortunately, this is common. I constantly see cap rates and cash on cash returns listed as the same percentage. I say to myself, "Okay, either this real estate agent doesn't know how to calculate the numbers or he truly thinks they are the same thing." Either scenario is pretty scary. You must know how to calculate returns to make sure that the numbers presented by the seller or the listing agent are accurate.

They Add Unguaranteed Income To The Financials In Order To Justify A Higher Asking Price

Many NNN leased properties contain a percentage rent clause in the lease agreement. Sometimes, the real estate agent will add in extra rental income from the percentage rent clause to justify a higher asking price for the property.

I struggle with this one. On one hand it is a valid point that the income did come in, therefore the NOI was higher, which increases the property's value. On the other hand, it is not guaranteed income. A breakpoint has to be met to get that bonus rental income. While the breakpoint may have been previously achieved, there is no guarantee that it will continue to do so in the future.

If there is adequate history that the breakpoint has consistently been met year after year, then add the income in. However, you do not want to add in extra income to the NOI if the breakpoint has not been previously achieved on a regular basis and the listing agent is merely guessing that it will happen in the future. If you do calculate in this bonus income into the NOI, I personally wouldn't add in the full amount. Unless the income can be guaranteed, it doesn't have the same value as other income that is guaranteed.

They Use Unrealistic Proposed Financing Scenarios

As of today, you will find that the Wall Street Journal Prime rate is 8.25%. However, you will see many commercial property listings with proposed financing at a 6.50% interest rate. With the high price of commercial real estate, that 1.75% mortgage interest rate difference will make a HUGE impact to your cash on cash return. The listing agent may post an unrealistic interest rate in the proposed financing section to make the property look like it cash flows, when it doesn't.

Real estate agents may also put into the proposed financing section, amortization schedules that are unrealistic as well. For instance, they may use a 30 year, interest only, financing scenario for a retail strip property or office building, when those terms are only available when purchasing apartment buildings.

Sometimes the property's numbers are so bad, that this is the only way to make the property more attractive to an investor than it is. I think this is really stupid for an agent to do. Here's why. What will happen is that an uneducated real estate investor will come along, tie the property up with a purchase contract, and then fail to close because he couldn't find financing with suitable terms. The real estate investor may have been fooled, but the lender won't be. Why, as a real estate agent or seller, would you waste your time?

They Post A Picture Of The Property That Is Not The Actual Property

What if you saw a picture posted on a dating website that had the following disclaimer; "Photo is not the actual person." It would make you wonder what that person has to hide. It's the same thing in real estate. Why would a real estate agent use a photo of a different property unless there is something to hide? Unless, the project is under construction, there should be a picture of the actual property in the offering package.

Be Aware Of Those Real Estate Agents Who Use The Phrase "Principals Only"

Be aware of real estate agents who advertise a listing with the phrase, "Principals Only" listed at the bottom. Essentially, what the listing agent is saying here is, "If I have to split my commission with another real estate agent, I don't even want to look at your offer."

> What if you saw a picture posted on a dating website that had the following disclaimer; "Photo is not the actual person." It would make you wonder what that person has to hide. It's the same thing in real estate.

Do you know what this says about the real estate agent? It says, "I can care less about you, Mr. Seller. All I care about is my commission. I want it ALL!" I think it's a bunch of crap. It kind of reminds me of behavior that I sometimes see with my four year old son. A real estate agent, by law, must present ALL written offers to the seller, no matter who it comes from.

Most sellers aren't aware of this common practice, and so it continues. Watch for this when you decide to sell your first commercial property.

They Want A Cut Of The Deal, In Addition To Their Commission

I've never had this happen to me, but I just read a comment online from a real estate investor whose commercial real estate agent was insisting on a percentage of the development's sales (see equity participation in the financing section), in addition to his normal commission. I find that completely out of line. I would have responded, "How does it feel to want?"

THE REAL ESTATE PURCHASE CONTRACT

Now that all of *that* is out of the way, let's go into the detail of the real estate contract. With your real estate agent on board, you will be ready to make a written offer on the property.

There Is No Standard Purchase Contract

If you were to buy a commercial property in California, you would find the commercial real estate purchase contract used by Realtors to be an eleven page document. If you went to Ohio, the commercial real estate purchase contract used by Realtors is a three page document. So, which one is standard? Neither and both. There's probably some valid things that the Ohio purchase contract should contain, that it doesn't and the California purchase contract is probably overkill. The point is, there is no standard purchase contract. You can add or subtract anything that is on a "standard" contract form to include whatever works for both parties.

Chapter Eight

You Can Agree To Almost Anything

The seller and purchaser can agree to almost anything in a purchase contract. If you decide that the seller must take you to dinner on Friday night, and both parties agree, then that is an obligation the seller must fulfill. I know that is a crazy example, but you get my point here. You can customize any purchase contract to meet your specific situation.

Never Offer The Asking Price

Never offer the asking price for a property. It's called the asking price for a reason. There are a few exceptions to this rule, but not many. If you are not embarrassed by your offer, then you have offered too much money. You are not looking for a good deal. You are looking for a great deal. In doing this, there is the risk that you may "offend" the seller. If the seller is truly motivated, he will be grateful to get any offer at all. There are just too many other commercial properties for sale to be working with sellers who are not truly motivated to sell their property.

When a low written offer is presented to the listing agent, he may say, "This offer is way too low. I know the seller won't accept that price." Real estate agents are legally obligated to present all written purchase offers to the seller. Sometimes, they need to be gently reminded of that fact.

Money Makes It Legal

Until money or "something of value" changes hands, the purchase contract may have the signature of the seller and the buyer, but it would not be legally binding. It is that "something of value" that makes the purchase contract legally binding. Ask me how I know that! Let me tell you another nice little story...

I found a really great vacant retail building located in Anderson, Indiana listed for sale on eBay. The seller and I agreed upon a purchase price, then we signed all of the purchase agreements via fax. I asked the seller if he wanted me to send the earnest deposit at that time, or if it was okay to wait until I flew out there for the inspection which was scheduled for the upcoming weekend. It would take about the same amount of time for it to get there either way. He told me to just bring the earnest deposit with me when I came out for the inspection.

> The seller knew, because we hadn't exchanged the earnest deposit, that we technically did not have a legally binding contract.

Well, that was my big mistake. Once I got to Anderson the seller's partner decided because they had just received a Letter of Intent (LOI) from a possible tenant, that the value of the building was worth $150,000 more than the price we had agreed upon. The seller knew, because we hadn't exchanged the earnest deposit, that we technically did not have a legally binding contract. I knew it too. I was so mad at myself. I had to decide if the property was worth the extra money or if I should walk away from the deal before the inspection even took place. I decided that the building was still worth purchasing, even at the increased cost and proceeded with the inspection.

So, if you go through the effort of agreeing upon a price and signing the purchase contract, get the earnest deposit to the seller, or his real estate agent, ASAP.

MAKE THE CONTRACT AS SPECIFIC AS POSSIBLE

Let's go over some of the details of the specific items in the purchase contract that you will need to keep your eye on.

Purchaser's Name

You should put your name down as the purchaser followed with "and/or assigns." For instance, I would write it like this: "Monica Villasenor and/or assigns." This enables the purchase contract to be assignable, when it otherwise would not be. Assigning a commercial real estate purchase contract is not as common in commercial real estate transactions, as it is in residential real estate transactions. It's just nice to have the flexibility in case you need it. If the seller questions you about it, just say that you plan on closing the property in one of your corporate names. You need to consult with your attorney to decide which one it will be. That explanation should appease the seller.

Property Description

The property address and parcel number must be correct. If you sign a purchase contract with the wrong address or parcel number, you are not in contract to purchase the property.

Earnest Deposit

Remember, the exchange of money or something of value is what makes the purchase contract legally binding. The seller's real estate agent will generally list the earnest deposit amount the seller would like to have accompany any purchase offer. However, you don't have to offer that exact amount of money specified. The earnest deposit is just another aspect of the deal that can be negotiated.

The amount of the earnest deposit is usually a bigger issue for the real estate agent than it is for the seller. However, the real estate agent should not be concerned with the amount of the earnest deposit, until the price and the terms of the property have been negotiated and accepted by the seller. I don't like having my money out of my hands, so I'm willing to provide only a $5,000 earnest deposit when I'm purchasing properties priced at $1,500,000 or less.

Financing Terms

If you are going to apply for conventional commercial real estate financing you will need to specify the exact loan terms that you would find acceptable. For instance, if you will need a 7% interest only loan, amortized over 30 years, those terms better be written in the purchase contract. If you just write the contract as being "contingent upon financing," with nothing specific regarding acceptable loan terms, then you will still be obligated to close the property, even if the loan terms the lender offers you, are unfavorable. If you do not close on the property, then you would lose your earnest deposit because the loan terms were not specifically spelled out. If the seller has agreed to carry a mortgage, those specific terms should be spelled out in the contract as well. You don't want any financial surprises at the closing table.

The approval and funding process takes a loooong time when obtaining a loan from a conventional commercial real estate lender. It is not unusual for the loan to take over six months to close. A commercial real estate appraisal itself, can take four to six weeks to complete. Make sure you have allotted yourself enough time in the purchase contract to secure financing.

Due Diligence

The *due diligence* time frame is where you will decide whether the property does or does not work for you. We will go into great depths about due diligence in Chapter 9. What you need to know at this point, is that during the due diligence period, you will receive all of the information from the seller that you will need to complete your evaluation of the property. This information may include a copy of the actual lease agreements, the property's financial reports, and inspections already performed. Additionally, all the inspections that are needed, such as the on site physical inspection, environmental reports, and pest inspections will need to be performed.

There is a certain amount of time specified in the purchase contract to complete your due diligence. However, if the seller is not cooperating with providing you with the necessary information, in a timely fashion, then the due diligence time frame starts from the date when you received the missing information from the seller.

Contingencies

Contingencies are your escape clauses. We discussed one of them above, which is financing. You have a certain number of days, as per the purchase contract, to perform all of your due diligence and meet all of your obligations (assuming the seller has meet his). After that period of time, you will either need to sign off that the contingencies have been met or cancel the purchase agreement (in writing, of course).

Sometimes it's the seller, not the purchaser, who wants to cancel the purchase contract. This happened to me with the condo conversion property. The property was listed for sale at $1,680,000. We locked the property up for $1,520,000. In the meantime, while we were doing our due diligence, the seller received a full price back up offer. The seller started moving quite slowly in getting the necessary information to us that we needed to complete our due diligence. The seller's real agent told us, "You are past your due diligence time frame and the contract is not good anymore."

We adamantly disagreed. We replied, "The seller has failed to provide the information that he is obligated to give us. Our time frame does not start until we have received the information that we are entitled to." We had to threaten legal action if the seller failed to close the property. Eventually, we received the missing information and closed on the property. Although, the seller never came out and said, "Hey, I want to cancel the transaction." his actions spoke loud and clear.

Closings Costs

Which closing costs is the buyer responsible to pay and which closing costs is the seller responsible to pay? Generally, in each region, there are once again "standards" of which party pays which closing costs. Does it really matter? It depends. If the regional standards are slanted in your favor, as the buyer, then I would go with the standard. If not, then the closing costs, are just another item that will have to be negotiated with the seller. There really is no harm in asking the seller to pay all of your closing costs. If the seller agrees to this, be aware that your lender may put a limit on how much money the seller is able to contribute to your closing costs.

Items Included In The Sale

If there is something that is unique located on the property that you wish to make part of the deal, make sure it's included in the sale. Sometimes there will be items on the property site that belong to the existing tenants, that the seller has no right to include in the purchase. Also think about items that you may want removed at the seller's expense. For instance, let's say that you are purchasing a vacant building which has a large sign on site from the previous tenant. The city may mandate that you take the sign down, which could be a large expense. In that case, you would request the seller to remove the sign at his expense. Make sure what is or is not included is clearly detailed in the purchase contract.

To sum it up, everything regarding the purchase contract must be in writing. It doesn't matter what was discussed between the seller and the purchaser. If it's not in the purchase contract, just forget it was even said. It's your job to get EVERYTHING in writing.

CLAUSES TO ADD TO THE PURCHASE CONTRACT THAT WILL FINANCIALLY PROTECT YOU

There are certain clauses that you can write into your purchase agreement that may prove extremely beneficial to you. The sky is the limit on potential clauses that are out there, but I'm only giving you the four clauses that I have found to be helpful with my personal commercial real estate transactions.

1. "This purchase agreement is subject to approval from the purchaser's (insert person here)."

This person can be an attorney, your partner, your cat, whoever you want to put down in the purchase contract. This clause gives you, the purchaser, another way out of the deal if needed. If everything looks good, but you decide to change your mind at a later point, it could be your "attorney" who advised you not to move forward with the deal.

2. "Purchaser has the right to review and approve a potential tenant before any formal lease agreement is signed."

This is a STRONG clause. When you are in contract to purchase a property, you have an interest in the property. You don't want the seller signing an unfavorable, long term lease with a tenant, while you are in contract to purchase that property.

If you are looking to purchase apartments, then the seller or the property management company may not screen tenants quite as well as usual or they may place tenants in the units with a long term lease at whatever rental amount they want. This happened to me with the condo conversion property. The market rental rate was around $595-$625/month for each unit. Once we had the property under contract, the seller's management company started putting tenants in the units for $525/month. What made this situation particularly bad, was that it was illegal for me to raise their rents due to the condo conversion.

This situation also came into play with the Indiana property. The seller showed me the LOI from a potential tenant, which was the owner of a car dealership business. The rental rate offered from the potential tenant was WAY below the market rental rate, which I found unacceptable. Because I was in contract to purchase the property, and had put this clause in the purchase contract, the seller could not have signed the tenant's formal lease agreement without my written permission. I told the seller that if he signed the lease with the tenant, I would not purchase the property. I felt having the tenant in the property, at that absurd rental rate, was worse than purchasing the property vacant.

3. "Seller shall leave all vacant units rent ready."

I messed up with not having this clause in the purchase contract not once, but twice. The first time was when I was buying my Ohio apartments. I didn't even think about it at the time. Once we were in contract to purchase the property, the seller was less than motivated to spend her own money to get the vacant units ready to rent. I was out of state and didn't go back to ensure that they were rent ready. Even if I had, I did not have this clause in the contract anyway. Immediately after the property closed, I had to pay to completely rehab four of the units.

The second time I failed to put this clause in the purchase contract was when I bought the condo conversion property. I actually remembered to tell my real estate agent to add this clause to the purchase contract. However, I failed to check to make sure it was in there. It wasn't. Once again, in addition to the insult of having some of the units rented at below market rental rates, all of the vacant units were needing major work. I was just so pissed off at myself for making this mistake AGAIN!

4. "The earnest deposit shall be returned to the buyer at the buyer's request, without the seller's written authorization. Doing so shall render the purchase contract

null and void."

I honestly haven't tried this one yet. But, I have good reason to want this clause in the purchase contract. I've had two occasions where I did not go through with the purchase of a property and had trouble with getting the seller to sign the paperwork necessary for the title company to release my earnest deposit. The most memorable time, and not in a good way, was with the Indiana deal. The purchase contract was contingent upon securing financing in the amount of $1,200,000. I was able to secure only a $1,000,000 loan. We would have still continued with the purchase if the seller would have agreed to carry the $200,000 difference. He opted to take a back up offer instead. I didn't blame him, as I would have done the same thing.

I told him, "Being mad does not entitle you to my money." He would have been content to see the money sit in the escrow account as long as I didn't get it.

The seller refused to sign the paperwork that would allow the title company to return my earnest deposit. The problem was, the seller was mad at me because he had paid for the appraisal-an expense that would have been reimbursed to him at closing. Nothing was put into writing about what would happen in the event that escrow did not close. I told him, "Being mad does not entitle you to my money." He would have been content to see the money sit in the escrow account, as long as I didn't get it. He spoke to me of honoring what we discussed. The seller and his partner were the same people who jacked the price of the property up $150,000 on me when we had already signed the purchase contract, and they were

143

talking to me about honoring agreements!

After months of deliberations, the seller agreed to $500 and the remaining $4,500 would be returned to me. I would have fought it to the end, mostly because I'm stubborn, but also because I was legally right. I refused to back down because of it.

These are just a few of the many, many different clauses that you can put into a purchase contract to financially protect yourself. I'm sure that with each commercial real estate transaction you do, you will learn even more clauses that will financially protect you. Hopefully, you will learn your "lessons" the first time and not mess up twice, like I did.

WRITE THE PURCHASE CONTRACT IN A WAY THAT WILL REDUCE YOUR DOWN PAYMENT

I think we can all agree that coming up with the down payment is our biggest obstacle in purchasing commercial real estate. We need to do everything that we can to find ways to reduce that down payment amount. Here are a couple of suggestions.

Have The Seller Cover Your Closing Costs

The easiest way to come into a real estate deal with less money is to have the seller cover your closing costs. It happens all the time in residential real estate, so there's no reason not to do it with commercial real estate too. Generally, a lender will allow the seller to pay up to six percent of the purchase price towards the buyer's closing costs. If the seller does not agree to this, just increase the purchase price by the amount that your closing costs will be and then have the seller cover the closing costs. The seller nets the same amount of money. The contract is just written differently.

For example, if you are purchasing a commercial property for $1,000,000, you would increase the purchase price to $1,060,000 and have the seller pay $60,000 of your closing costs. The seller is still receiving his $1,000,000 and you will come in with a lot less money out of your pocket. To take advantage of this scenario, the property would have to appraise for the higher purchase price.

Repair Credits

Let's say that after you perform the property inspection, you discover items that need to be repaired (and there will be). The seller does not want to spend the money to fix those items, but you won't purchase the property for the agreed upon price if you have to fix those items out of your own pocket. To satisfy both parties, the seller can give you a repair credit to compensate for those repairs. Those items will then be fixed, after closing, by the purchaser. Lenders, once again, have a say on how much they will allow for repair credits.

Ask The Seller To Carry A Second Mortgage

If the seller is willing to carry a second mortgage, this will allow you to come in with less money. Even something as small as a five percent second mortgage, can allow you to come in with $50,000 less on a $1,000,000 property. That's a lot of money that you can put towards the purchase of another commercial property.

Chapter Eight

Questionable Options

I don't want to go into anything that may be considered questionable or illegal. What I will say, is that sometimes the seller and purchaser agree to things that are settled after the property closes. If you chose to do this, be aware that certain transactions or agreements made "outside of escrow" can be considered fraudulent.

WHAT NOBODY TELLS YOU

1. Real estate agents don't necessarily know any more about commercial real estate investing than you do. They are usually only concerned with collecting a commission.
2. Signing a purchase contract does not obligate you to purchase the property.
3. There is no "standard" purchase contract.
4. Verbal agreements don't mean anything.
5. The earnest deposit does not have to be the amount the listing agent specifies.
6. There are ways to write a purchase contract that enables you to come to the closing table with less money.
7. There are many special clauses that you can put in the purchase contract to financially protect yourself.
8. Real estate transactions, often get personal, despite what is written in the purchase contract.

THE DUE DILIGENCE PROCESS

G et out your investigator hat! Due diligence is the time to put your investigation skills to the test. Due diligence is a term used to describe the process of the detailed analysis and research you will perform on the property and it's financials. You have performed quite a bit of analysis on the property just to get to this point. However, you did not have all of the information you needed from the seller until this phase. Nor did you have the necessary property inspections and reports completed that will allow you to understand exactly what you are buying. This is the time that you will look for any "skeletons in the closet."

INSPECTIONS

You Must Do An Inspection

You must, must, must do an inspection. It's just a cost of doing business. Try to put the cost of the inspection into perspective. It will not cost you a lot of money to pay for the inspection, it will cost you a lot of money if you don't. My first experience with having a property inspection performed on a commercial property was for an apartment building located in Cincinnati, Ohio. The cost of the inspection was $1,200. There were additional costs such as the airfare, the car rental, and the hotel, as well.

The property looked great on paper. However, when I personally visited the property, it was a complete disaster. Many of the units had seriously dangerous living conditions such as exposed wires, water leaks accompanied by mold growth, and inoperable air conditioning units.

The property owner was the definition of slum lord. As we went from unit to unit, tenants told us numerous stories about how they had asked the landlord to fix certain items, but they never were fixed. One of those tenants was a young mom (and I mean young) who had a newborn baby. Her apartment, which only contained a bed in the middle of the living room, was extremely hot because her air conditioning unit wasn't working. She said she had complained about it, but nothing was done. We actually went out and bought a fan for her.

The worst apartment unit I experienced that day was occupied by an elderly gentleman who couldn't control his bowels. There was feces everywhere! The stench was so dense, I literally couldn't walk into his apartment without gagging. Being pregnant at the time couldn't have helped much. It was just a sad situation.

I wanted to purchase the property just to correct those poor tenant's living situation, but I couldn't. The property was just too expensive considering it's condition. At that point, I did the only thing I could for the tenants, which was to forward the inspection report to the city's building department. I don't know if anything was ever done about the building's hazardous living conditions, or not.

Although I spent $1,200 for the property inspection, it saved me from purchasing a property that would have cost hundreds of thousands of dollars to fix. It was money well spent.

Keep Your Personal Living Standards Out Of The Picture

A month later, I was in contract to purchase the apartments in Windham, Ohio. By that time, I was eight months pregnant. My husband was not very happy about the fact that I was flying across country late in my pregnancy to participate in the inspection-but there was no way I was going to let him do it for me. He wouldn't be able to be objective with the property. He wouldn't be able to keep his personal living standards out of the picture.

It is essential to always remain objective during the inspection process. You will be absolutely flabbergasted by how some people choose to live. It's so easy to pass your personal living standards onto others, but you can't do that. You must try to look past the tenant's way of living and focus on the physical structure of the building.

> **We had just started the inspection when the seller said, "These units are great. They have no deferred maintenance." As she said that, the inspector was finding all kinds of items that needed repaired.**

Never **Believe What The Seller Tells You**

On the day of the inspection in Windham, Ohio, I was

met at the property by the inspector and the seller. We had just started the inspection when the seller said, "These units are great. They have no deferred maintenance." As she said that, the inspector was finding all kinds of items which needed repaired. On the seller's defense, sometimes a tenant will not report items that need to be repaired to their landlord or management company. However, that is the exception, not the rule.

With these units I could see that the physical building structure was in fairly good condition. The property would require some work, but not a complete overhaul. Upon receiving the inspection report, we were able to come up with a figure for the repair costs. The inspection report was used to renegotiate the purchase contract with the seller, which resulted in a $60,000 repair credit. Without that repair credit, I wouldn't have had enough money to close the property. That inspection cost me $1,500, but also saved me $60,000.

Pay Close Attention To The Age Of The Building's Mechanical Systems

The building's mechanical systems such as it's HVAC unit, plumbing, electrical, and other mechanical components of the building may be beyond their useful life. If you are inspecting an 30 unit apartment building and all of the hot water heaters are beyond their useful life, you will have to pay a ton of money to replace them. How is the asphalt? How is the concrete? Will you have to remove any trees because it's roots are cracking the property's foundation? How old are the roofs? How old are the windows? Are they single pane? Are the original appliances still being used in the units? You don't want to close on a property and then be surprised by having to replace the property's major operating systems. Those large expenses can be financially devastating if you aren't prepared for them!

Were Improvements Or Repairs Done Correctly?

If the seller reports that a major repair or replacement was done within the last few years, you will also need to ensure that it was done correctly. For instance, on the condo conversion property, the seller reported that all of the roofs were replaced four years before. However, my dad, who owned his own roofing business for over 30 years, drove by the property and told me, "Those roofs were not installed by a roofing contractor." "How do you know?" I asked. "The nails they used are too long. They also did not use enough nails for each shingle. There should be four nails per shingle. There's only three" he clarified. Instead of having to replace the roof in 20-25 years, it will need to be replaced in about five years because it was done in a manner that jeopardized the roof's normal useful life.

ENVIRONMENTAL REPORTS

With certain types of commercial properties, you will need to have an environmental report performed to protect yourself. While there is a significant cost for these reports, they are worth having done because of the protection they provide. Just like the property inspection, you don't want any financial surprises, like being responsible to clean up an environmental problem on a property you own, despite the fact that you didn't cause it.

Environmental reports are classified as either Phase I, Phase

II, or Phase III. Whether you need an environmental report, and which type, will depend upon what type of building you are buying. For instance, gas stations need an in-depth environmental report to make sure that there has been no gasoline leaking into the ground from the gasoline tanks. Many times, the seller will have an environmental report already done, so he will know of any environmental issues prior to selling the property.

SURVEY

A survey shows the boundaries of the property and the improvements located on the property. It allows you to verify what you are buying. A survey may uncover certain problems, such as discovering that a neighbor's fence is located on the subject property. If there are things located on the property that are not supposed to be there, a survey will discover it.

REVIEW THE PAPERWORK

REVIEW EXISTING LEASE AGREEMENTS

You probably did not have the actual lease agreements to analyze before you were under contract to purchase the property. But now that you are in contract, the seller will supply you with a copy of all existing lease agreements. You will need to go through each one of them with a fine tooth comb. You are going to be taking over the lease agreements, as they are written. You must know to what you are agreeing. You also want to verify that everything corresponds to what the seller reported. Review each lease agreement a minimum of three times to ensure that you don't miss anything.

Does The Rental Rate On The Lease Agreement Match The Rental Rate Indicated On The Rent Roll?

Sometimes the seller may report a certain rental rate amount on the rent roll, which may not match the rental rate in the tenant's lease agreement. This was the case, when I was in contract to purchase the apartments in Windham, Ohio. I wanted to make sure that it was an innocent error and that the higher rental rate indicated on the rent roll was the correct amount. If the higher rental rate on the rent roll is correct, where is the documentation the tenant signed acknowledging the rental rate increase?

This situation doesn't come into play much with retail or office properties. The tenants are going to be more stable, but you will still want to make sure that the rental rate in their lease agreement corresponds with what the seller reported. Is the tenant's rental space size in the lease agreement correct? Is the rental rate per square foot correct? Do the tenants pay CAM fees? Does the lease agreement termination date match? Are many of the tenant's lease agreements scheduled to terminate at the same time? Verify who pays which property expenses.

You should have all of your outstanding questions answered through reviewing the lease documents. If you find something in the lease agreement that does not match what the seller reported, it's a valid reason for the purchase contract to be renegotiated.

Chapter Nine

Does The Security Deposit On The Lease Agreement Match What Is Listed By The Seller?

Just as you verified the tenant's rental rate, you will also need to verify the tenant's security deposit. When the property closes, the tenant's security deposits will be transferred to you in the form of a credit against your closing costs. It is not unusual, especially when purchasing apartments, to have changes to the rent role every month. You may request that the seller provide you with a tenant estoppel. A *tenant estoppel* is a form that the tenant must sign, in which the tenant acknowledges their rental rate and their security deposit on file. Having a tenant estoppel form signed by all tenants makes everything clear for all parties.

Unusual Items

You want to make sure there is nothing unusual stated in the lease which may have a negative financial implication for you. For instance, do you see a provision in the lease that gives the tenant an improvement allowance for a certain period of time, which would decrease the property's future income?

Unusual items found in the lease agreements aren't always bad. Sometimes there's something unexpected in the lease agreement which just sweetens the deal. For example, what if you found that a tenant was supposed to be paying CAM fees and had not been? After you closed on the property, you could collect those outstanding CAM fees, providing you with extra income you would otherwise not have received. Or, what if you see that a rental rate review could have been performed every year for a tenant who has a below market rental rate, but it's never been performed? After closing, you could increase the tenant's rental rate to the market rental rate, providing more income to you.

REVIEW THE EXISTING FINANCIALS

The seller should also provide you with the detailed financial reports of the property. This should include not only a Profit/Loss Statement, but also the seller's portion of his personal or business tax return that corresponds to the property (usually a Schedule E). It is so easy to manipulate the numbers on a Profit/Loss statement, by removing or lowering expenses, to make the property look like it's more valuable than it is.

Cross checking the Profit/Loss Statement against the seller's tax return will help you catch sneaky accounting. They won't match exactly, but they should be fairly close. If you don't know how to do this, have your CPA or bookkeeper do this for you. It wouldn't take long and the cost would be minimal. It's a small price to pay to make sure you are purchasing a property that is financially performing as the seller has indicated.

CONTACT THE LOCAL GOVERNMENT OFFICIALS (CITY OR COUNTY)

Call the building department in the city where the property is located to verify that there are no outstanding violations on the property. You will also want to make sure that the property is zoned what you think it is zoned. This is important for a retail building because certain businesses are prohibited in certain zoning classifications, which would reduce your ability to rent the property. It takes a long time for a prospective tenant to get a rezoning approval or a special use permit, if they are even able to get an approval at all.

I found out the importance of contacting the local city officials with the Indiana property. The prospective tenant who submitted the LOI was the owner of a car dealership business. I spoke to a city official who told me that the city was not happy with that particular business owner. The city had granted him a special use permit to hold a car sale at the subject property's site. The special use permit was issued with an understanding that the business owner must stop parking the vehicles he sells at his regular place of business in a certain spot. After the sale, he ignored the city's request and continued parking the cars for sale in the same location. The city wasn't happy that he had not lived up to his side of the agreement. That was one strike against him.

Another issue the city had was that this particular building was in a really great retail area. They were not overly enthusiastic about seeing another car dealership in the area. With that information, I did not believe the prospective tenant was going to be able to get the rezoning request approved. Had I not called the city officials, I wouldn't have that information.

BACKING OUT OF THE CONTRACT

After your due diligence is complete, you will have enough information to figure out whether you would like to proceed forward with the purchase of the property or not. If you do not wish to proceed forward with the purchase, for any reason, you will need to cancel the purchase contract in writing.

Sometimes the seller's real estate agent has a form that has to be signed. Other times, you can just type up a letter and have your real estate agent forward it to the seller's real estate agent. As long as you stay within the written parameters of the purchase contract you should be able to cancel the agreement without any problem. However, my experience has shown, it's not always that easy. As mentioned before, both parties have to sign the paperwork for the title company to release your earnest deposit back to you.

WHAT NOBODY TELLS YOU

1. The due diligence process costs you money, but it will save you more money than you ever spend.
2. *Never* trust what the seller tells you.
3. It's up to you to ensure that the property's financials are correct.
4. You may find favorable or unfavorable surprises in the lease agreements.
5. The local government officials can be a great source of information about a property.

CHAPTER 10
FINANCING

Most real estate investors will not be paying cash to purchase commercial real estate. They will rely upon obtaining a loan to purchase a piece of commercial real estate. You have gone through a lot of work to get to this point. All of the work you have done, will be of no value, if you are unable to secure financing for the property.

When I went to finance my first commercial property, I assumed everything regarding the commercial real estate lending process was the same as it is with the residential real estate lending process. Just to stay consistent, I was wrong again.

Everything you may know about qualifying for a residential real estate loan, you can throw out the window. Qualifying for a commercial real estate loan is completely the opposite of qualifying for a residential real estate loan.

Chapter Ten

COMMERCIAL REAL ESTATE FINANCING OPTIONS

My husband, Mike, was concerned with our ability to obtain construction financing for the condo conversion project. I told him something that all of you should know as well. There's always money available to finance commercial real estate. It's just a matter of how much it's going to cost you. When I talk about the cost of a real estate loan, I'm referring to the points and the interest rate the lender charges.

> There's always money available to finance commercial real estate. It's just a matter of how much it's going to cost you.

There are many different types of real estate lenders who offer loans to purchase commercial real estate. Each of these different types of commercial real estate lenders will charge different points and interest rates. The different types of commercial real estate financing options that we will go into detail with include:

1. Conventional Commercial Real Estate Lenders
2. Seller Financing
3. Other Loan Options

There are also certain types of commercial real estate loans that we will not go into, such as Mezzanine and Bridge financing. These types of real estate loans usually come into play with more sophisticated commercial real estate deals, which you would rarely use during your first few commercial real estate deals.

160

CONVENTIONAL COMMERCIAL REAL ESTATE LENDERS

HOW COMMERCIAL REAL ESTATE LOANS ARE DIFFERENT FROM RESIDENTIAL REAL ESTATE LOANS

The Property Is The Primary Criteria For The Loan Approval

With a residential real estate loan, the lender will look at your financial strength, as the primary criteria for loan approval. With a commercial real estate loan, the property's cash flow from it's tenants is the primary lending criteria. As the borrower, your financial strength is a smaller, secondary criteria. The lender's primary concern is the ability to be paid back. The lender knows that you, as an individual, will not have the financial resources to carry the large mortgage payments associated with commercial real estate. They know that the tenants, who occupy the premise, will essentially be paying the mortgage.

It is *so* ingrained in residential real estate investor's minds that their *own* financial strength is everything, that they have not even thought it to be possible to move up to investing in commercial real estate. Not only is it possible, it's easier!

In essence, a real estate investor with a low credit score would probably be able to purchase a commercial property easier than they could purchase a residential property. This is an amazing concept that most real estate investors are not aware of. It is so ingrained in residential real estate investor's minds that their own financial strength is everything, that they have not even thought it to be possible to move up to investing in commercial real estate. Not only is it possible, it's easier!

Loan To Value (LTV) Levels Are Less

The borrower on a commercial real estate loan will be required to come into the deal with a higher percentage down payment, than the borrower on a residential real estate loan. A simple 5% difference in the down payment on a commercial property can be a staggering amount of money. For instance, if you had to come up with a 20% down payment, instead of a 15% down payment on a $2,000,000 property, that is an extra $100,000. That's a lot of money. Most people don't have any extra $100,000 just sitting in the bank.

Finding money for the down payment seems to be the major barrier for most real estate investors who want to purchase commercial real estate. This obstacle can be overcome. We will discuss ways to find money for the down payment in the next chapter.

Commercial Real Estate Loans Will Have A Higher Interest Rate Than Residential Real Estate Loans

Typically, you will find that the interest rate for commercial real estate loans will be 1-2% higher than the interest rate for residential real estate loans. This isn't always the case, such as when the loan will be used to purchase a building occupied by a A+, corporate guaranteed, long term tenant, but it is true the majority of the time.

Commercial Real Estate Lenders Charge Higher Points

Commercial real estate lenders will charge the borrower one to four points of the loan amount for providing the financing. If there are any mortgage broker fees, they will be added on top of the lender fees. Be aware of this, as it will affect how much money you will need to come up with in order to close the loan. The number of broker and lender points will be on the commitment letter that the lender forwards to you at the time your commercial real estate loan is approved.

Commercial Real Estate Loans May Have A Lock Out And/Or A Prepayment Penalty

Commercial real estate loans are extremely complex. Just as you had a lot of factors to evaluate, so will the lender. Most commercial real estate lenders want to make sure their loans are around for a while. Especially for the fact that it takes a lot more work to underwrite (evaluate and approve) commercial real estate loans, than it takes to underwrite residential real estate loans. To ensure that the loan is not paid off quickly, the lender may give you the option or they may mandate that the loan has a lock out provision. Typically, the lender will offer you a lower interest rate if you agree to a lockout.

A *prepayment penalty* and a *lockout* although two different things, are often confused as being the same thing. A prepayment penalty means that you can prepay the note, but there will be a fee to do so. A lock out means that you CAN NOT prepay the loan. If you do, all of the principal and interest payments you would have paid to the lender during the lockout period, *in addition to* the prepayment penalty, would be assessed.

For instance, if your commercial real estate loan has a 24 month lockout period and you want to refinance the loan after 12 months, then you would have to increase the amount of the new loan to cover the 12 months of payments remaining on the lock out period.

A lock out option needs to be thought through very carefully. Sometimes it's worth it. Most of the time, it's not.

Many Commercial Real Estate Loans Are Nonrecourse

Many times a commercial real estate loan will be a nonrecourse loan. This means you can give the lender the keys to the property and walk away with no personal recourse to you. The lender must feel very strongly about the strength of the tenant and the property's cash flow to offer a nonrecourse loan.

Most Commercial Real Estate Loans Are Assumable

It used to be that many residential loans were assumable. Now, they are not. However, the majority of commercial real estate loans are assumable. What a great selling feature! There is often an assumption fee of 1-2% of the loan balance. If a property has favorable assumable financing in place, the seller may be able to command a higher selling price, than if the purchaser had to obtain new financing at a higher market interest rate.

If your criteria can be met because of the property's existing, assumable financing, it may be a situation where it makes sense to pay the full asking price the property. Favorable financing can make a difference of thousands of dollars in cash flow, which goes straight to your pocket.

If you will be seeking new financing, make sure there is an assumption clause in the loan you obtain. That way you can offer this great feature to a buyer, down the road.

WHAT COMMERCIAL REAL ESTATE LENDERS LOOK FOR

One of the fantastic things about buying commercial real estate is that you, as the borrower, are a small factor in the lender's decision of whether or not they will approve your loan request. The lender will look at the income from the property to ensure it is adequate to cover the proposed payment. Yes, they will want to see your bank statements, credit report, and personal financial statement. Sometimes, they just need to have the information in order to put a check mark next to a box that says the papers are in the loan file. For the lender, approving a commercial real estate loan application is all about the property's numbers.

Debt Service Coverage Ratio

The *debt service coverage ratio* (DSCR) is a formula used by commercial real estate lenders that gives them a basis of whether the property is producing adequate income to pay the proposed loan payments. The DSCR is calculated by dividing the property's NOI by the proposed loan payments. For instance, if the property's NOI is $200,000, and the proposed yearly loan payments are $150,000, then the DSCR is 1.3.

$$\frac{\$200,000 \text{ NOI}}{\$150,000 \text{ Annual Mortgage Payments}} = 1.3 \text{ DSCR}$$

Most commercial real estate lenders want to see a DSCR of 1.2 or higher. In this case, the bank would most likely approve this loan because the DSCR is 1.3, which is higher than the required 1.2 DSCR. If a property has a .90 DSCR, then the loan simply won't be approved. It doesn't matter if you have a 750 credit score and a stable job. That's not what a commercial real estate lender cares about. They want to make sure that they will be able to be paid back. They can tell from this simple ratio, if that is likely to happen, or not.

TYPICAL LOAN TO VALUE (LTV) RATIOS ALLOWED BY COMMERCIAL REAL ESTATE LENDERS

When you were in the residential real estate investing world, you could find 95% or 100% LTV loan programs all day long. High LTV levels are not offered by commercial real estate lenders. This is one of the negative aspects of commercial real estate investing. You will have to come in with a higher down payment. However, that doesn't mean that the down payment has to be your own money.

There are always exceptions to the rule, but here are some general guidelines on what LTV and CLTV levels you can expect to borrow for the purchase of a commercial property. *Cumulative Loan To Value (CLTV)* is the total LTV of all the loans on a property, including any seller held financing. The typical LTV and CLTV levels commercial real estate lenders allow classified by property type, are as follows:

Multifamily   85% LTV
               95% CLTV

Retail/Office 75% LTV
              85% CLTV

Please remember, that these ratios are generally *maximum* levels. Each commercial property will be evaluated by the lender on a case by case basis, which may cause their acceptable LTV level to decrease.

POPULATION SIZE MATTERS

If a town's population size is small or the area is considered to be "rural," the lender may view it as a riskier loan. The LTV that the lender may be willing to allow, may decrease.

I learned that population size matters the hard way, when I applied for a loan to purchase the Windham, Ohio property. Windham has a whole population of 3,000 people. The lender dropped the amount of money they were willing to lend to me from 85% LTV to 60% LTV. That was a difference of $375,000. I was counting on a 85% LTV first mortgage from the lender, with a 10% seller held second mortgage. I was going to have a hard enough time coming up with the money to close the property with the 85% LTV first mortgage scenario. The seller was unwilling to carry the additional $375,000, so I was in a dilemma.

After much negotiation from my mortgage broker, the lender increased their loan to 75% LTV and the seller carried a 12% second mortgage. I came in with the remaining amount of money. This was one of those cases where my mortgage broker saved the day! He persuaded the lender and the seller to adjust their normal lending parameters to get the property closed. If you are buying a commercial property in a small town, please be aware that it's small population size can be a major lending obstacle.

FIXED OR ADJUSTABLE INTEREST RATE?

When I purchased my first commercial property, I really messed up on all aspects of obtaining financing. My choice of an adjustable interest rate was one of those mistakes. At the time, my biggest concern was cash flow. My goal was to have the lowest monthly payment possible. Another reason I chose to go with an adjustable interest rate mortgage was because the seller agreed to hold a second mortgage which contained a balloon payment due in three years. I would have to refinance the first mortgage to pay off the seller-held second mortgage within three years anyway.

After the first year, the interest rate increased 2%, raising my monthly mortgage payment by $2,000. I was netting a profit of $3,000/month. A decrease of $2,000/month, which was a 66% reduction in profit, really hurt! I would have been far better off to go with a fixed interest rate, even if initially it was a bit higher. That way, there wouldn't be any financial surprises down the road. You too, will need to decide if you would like a fixed interest rate mortgage or an adjustable interest rate mortgage. In order for you to make an educated decision, let's go over more information about interest rates.

HOW ARE ADJUSTABLE INTEREST RATES DETERMINED?

Adjustable interest rate commercial real estate loans are calculated by adding a certain percentage or a certain number of *basis points* to the prime rate. 100 basis points equals one percentage point. On the lender's term sheet, you may see the interest rate worded something like this; "Interest Rate = Prime + 300 basis points." However, to determine what the prime rate is, you would need to know which index the prime rate is based off of. Let's take a deeper look into the different indexes from which a prime rate can be based.

1. Wall Street Journal Prime Rate

This is the most widely used index in setting the interest rate for credit cards, home equity lines, automobile loans, and personal loans. From a borrower's perspective, this is not the index you want your commercial real estate loan to be based off of. It will have the highest interest rate compared to prime rates based off of other indexes. And yes, this is the "prime rate" that my interest rate for the loan on my Ohio property is based from.

2. Federated Funds Rate

This is the rate at which banks lend money to other banks.

3. Federal Discount Rate

This is the rate at which banks or other financial institutions may borrow directly from the Federal Reserve. The banks then lend the money to borrowers, at a higher interest rate, which is how they make the majority of their income.

Banks also borrow money from their customers. For instance, as of the date I'm writing this chapter (February, 2007), the Federal Discount Rate is 6.25%. There's not one bank I know of, that is offering a Certificate of Deposit which pays more than 5.85% interest. By borrowing money from it's customers, the bank is saving .40% on the cost of borrowing the money

169

from the Federal Reserve. This small percentage of savings may not seem like it would be worth the bank's effort. But when you are talking about millions of dollars, that .40% savings is A LOT of money.

4. LIBOR (London Interbank Offered Rate)

This is the index used in London, that is essentially equivalent to our Federated Funds Rate. **This is the index that you want your commercial loan based off of.**

5. The 11th District Cost of Funds

This index is often used with adjustable interest rate mortgages.

You can follow current index rates by going to www.bankrate.com.

> If you have two loan offers that seem identical, but one loan is based off of the Wall Street Journal Prime Rate and the other loan is based off of LIBOR, then those two "identical" loan offers are not even close to being the same.

WHY IS ALL OF THIS IMPORTANT TO KNOW?

Why do you need to know this? This is a book about commercial real estate investing, not banking, right? The whole point of investing in commercial real estate is to make money. In order to do that, you are taking advantage of the principal of leverage, by obtaining financing. You must look at reducing costs at every opportunity possible. The debt service (mortgage) on the property is usually one of the property's largest expenses. If you know why lenders charge the interest rates they do, then you will be able to make smarter decisions regarding which loan program to choose.

For instance, if you have two loan offers that seem identical, but one loan is based off of the Wall Street Journal Prime Rate and the other loan is based off of LIBOR, then those two "identical" loan offers are not even close to being the same.

Let's put a scenario into play to see which option is a better deal on a $1,000,000 loan.

Loan #1
Fixed Interest Rate 9%
30 Year Amortization
Monthly Payment $8,046.23
Yearly Payment $96,554.76

Loan #2
Adjustable Interest Rate 7%
Interest Only
Monthly Payment $5,833.33
Yearly Payment $69,999.96

The first year's difference between the two loans is $26,554.80, or over $2,000/month. This seems like a no-brainer. Take the adjustable interest rate loan and pocket all that extra money. However, after the first year, the interest rate increases 2%, which makes your yearly mortgage payment $90,000. Now, you are only saving $6,554.76 over the fixed interest rate option. The following year your yearly mortgage payment increases another 2% to $110,000. At this point, you are now paying $13,445.24/year more than the fixed interest rate loan.

So, which loan option is the better choice? You can't know for certain because you can't predict future interest rates.

There are a lot of factors to consider.

Until you have a couple of commercial properties under your belt, stick with a fixed interest rate mortgage. Especially right now, while the interest rates are still at an all time low. Then, after you have more experience, you will be able to analyze the risk versus reward of going with an adjustable interest rate loan. Remember too, that refinancing a commercial real estate loan is expensive. If you add the cost of refinancing into the equation, the extra money you would have made from going with an adjustable interest rate mortgage, may be completely wiped out.

THE COMMERCIAL REAL ESTATE LOAN PROCESS

The commercial real estate loan process is a long one. While it is pretty easy to have a residential real estate loan completed in under a month, it is not the case with a commercial real estate loan. There is a lot of due diligence to complete, including an appraisal, inspections, and reports that have to be ordered, completed, and reviewed before the lender can approve and fund the loan. Let's go through the commercial real estate loan process.

1. Contact A Commercial Mortgage Broker
2. Compile Information For The Loan Package
3. A Letter Of Interest (LOI) Is Issued
4. A Commitment Letter/Term Sheet Is Issued
5. The Appraisal And Inspections Are Ordered
6. Provide Additional Items The Lender May Require
7. Closing

As always, let's go into detail with each step.

1. CONTACT A COMMERCIAL MORTGAGE BROKER

Most of the time you will not be applying for a commercial real estate loan from your local bank. A local bank is usually not equipped to handle the large loan requests like the one you will be seeking. There are lenders with deep pockets who specialize in lending on commercial real estate. These are the types of lenders with which you should apply for a commercial real estate loan.

You will need the help of a REPUTABLE commercial real estate mortgage broker to guide you through the commercial real estate loan process. Seriously, I can't emphasize the importance of this enough. Commercial mortgage brokers know which lenders come through and which ones don't. They have the appropriate contacts with favorable lenders and can make the loan process a whole lot easier for you.

Commercial real estate lenders need to originate loans to stay in business. They rely heavily on loan applications submitted by commercial mortgage brokers. If your loan request doesn't fully comply with their lending parameters, the lender may fund your loan as a favor to your broker, when it may not have otherwise been approved.

Watch Out For The Crooks

Please note how I said it is important to work with a REPUTABLE commercial mortgage broker. There are so many crooked ones. Ask me how I know that! I certainly have worked with more than my fair share of them. The commercial mortgage business is a fairly unregulated

173

industry. Anyone can put up a website and call themselves a commercial mortgage broker. Just because a commercial mortgage broker has a website, doesn't mean they know what they are doing.

Unlike residential mortgage brokers, there is not a whole lot of protection from scrupulous commercial mortgage brokers. Maybe the government thinks that if you are sophisticated enough to be purchasing commercial real estate, then you should be sophisticated enough to watch your back for these types of people, too.

Commercial Mortgage Broker Points

Residential mortgage brokers are paid by the lender once the loan closes. However, points paid to commercial mortgage brokers are paid by the borrower when the loan closes. Commercial mortgage brokers typically earn one to five points on the loan amount. The number of points you agree to pay your commercial mortgage broker is important because it will affect how much money you will need to close the transaction. For instance, if your commercial mortgage broker charges two points on a $2,000,000 loan, it would cost you $40,000 which you must be prepared to pay at closing.

COMMON SCAMS AND TRICKS OF THE TRADE COMMERCIAL MORTGAGE BROKERS AND LENDERS DON'T WANT YOU TO KNOW ABOUT

Up-Front Fees

Sometimes a commercial mortgage broker will require that you send him $3,000-$20,000, just for the privilege of having him submit the loan package to different commercial real estate lenders, along with a document which states whether these up-front fees are refundable or non refundable.

These types of people are scam artists. What a mortgage broker is saying, when he requires money up-front is, "I may or may not be able to get this loan done for you. I may or may not even take the time to submit it to more than one lender. But either way, I get my money."

What a mortgage broker is saying, when he requires money up-front is, "I may or may not be able to get this loan done for you. I may or may not even take the time to submit it to more than one lender. But either way, I get my money."

For some "brokers," this is the only way they make money. A broker may say, "Oh, yeah. I can get the loan done. I can do it." The fact is, most of the time the loan he says he can do, will not fit your financing parameters, forcing you to decline the loan. Then, he will say, "I offered you a loan. You didn't take it, so the fees are non refundable." **Even if a mortgage broker or lender says that their fees are refundable, you will never see that money again!** It took me being screwed three times with these bogus, up-front fees, before I saw the light.

Even direct commercial real estate lenders can be bad in regards to charging up-front fees. I received a conditional loan approval from a lender who wanted a non refundable $10,000 underwriting fee, a $199 processing fee, a $250 loan servicing set-up fee, and a monthly loan servicing fee of $199. However, the fee schedule I found on the lender's website, was as follows:

	Lender's Conditional Approval Letter	Same Lender's Website
Underwriting Fee	$10,000	$895
Processing Fee	$199	$199
Loan Servicing Fee	$250	$250
Monthly Loan Servicing Fee	$199	$99

I guess these types of lenders throw out whatever fees they think you may be willing to pay, just to see if it flies.

You can view this conditional loan approval letter on my website, www.monicavillasenor.net.

This is the type of stuff you need to watch for. These are the kind of shady things that happen all the time with commercial mortgage brokers and lenders, which I can't warn you about any more strongly.

There's a lot of talk and no action with these people. If the lender truly want to do the deal, they will. If they start needing a few more days, then a few more days, then a few more days after that, they are "dancing," and you better start looking elsewhere for financing.

Mortgage Brokers Who Represent Themselves As The Direct Lender When They Are Not

Many mortgage brokers represent themselves as the direct lender, when they are not. They will talk to you about their "investors" as if they were the direct funding source for the loan, when all they are really doing is shopping your loan to direct lenders or to other mortgage brokers. As them flat out if they are the direct lender. There's a lot of dishonesty in this profession, if you can't already tell. It really is disgusting.

2. COMPILE INFORMATION FOR THE LOAN PACKAGE

The underwriting or approval process for commercial real estate loans takes a lot longer than it does for residential real estate loans because there are a lot more factors the underwriter must look at. Some of the necessary items that may be requested by the lender to be presented with the loan package are as follows:

Borrower's Personal Financial Statement

The lender wants to see that you have a decent financial statement. It is essentially your financial report card. It doesn't have to be great, but the higher your personal worth, the higher it tips the scale in your favor. The lender wants to see that you have your personal financial house in order. If you can't manage your personal finances, how will you handle the finances of a larger property?

Borrower's Credit Report

The lender wants to make sure that you are, who you say you are. They also want to make sure there are no surprises on your credit report that you failed to report to them. A good or excellent credit score is a bonus for the borrower, as it will probably result in a lower interest rate.

Chapter Ten

The Property's Profit/Loss Statement For The Last Two Years

You will have to get the Profit/Loss Statement of the property from the seller, unless you are refinancing a commercial property you already own. The lender will verify that the property's expenses are in line to what they should be.

Borrower's Resume

Are you new to real estate investing or are you a veteran real estate investor? Having experience as an real estate investor or as a real estate developer will make your loan package more attractive to the lender. Just as you would present yourself in the best light with a job resume, you should do the same thing for your real estate investment resume. You want to present yourself in a manner that shows the lender you are capable of owning and managing the property.

A Copy Of All Current Lease Agreements Associated With The Property

You will have obtained a copy of all the lease agreements from the seller during the due diligence process. The lender will go over the lease agreements like you did, to verify that the property's financials match what was reported. The lender will also ensure that the lease agreements don't contain bizarre clauses or conditions which would cause a large outlay of money in the future, thereby weakening the borrower's ability to make a mortgage payment in the future.

Executive Summary

An *executive summary* provides a one to five page summary

of the property. It allows the lender to get a picture of the property from a narrative point of view. Some of the items you may include in the executive summary are:

✓ Borrower Information
✓ Property Summary And Description
✓ Use Of Loan Funds
✓ Third Party Verifications
✓ Marketing Plan

Borrower's Tax Return For The Last Two Years

This one always worries me because the more real estate I purchase, the less income I show on my tax return due to real estate tax benefits, such as depreciation. Last year, I literally showed a loss of income, when I owned more than $4,500,000 of real estate.

Don't worry, like I do, about how much income your tax return shows you make. Commercial real estate loan underwriters are sharp. They will know why your income keeps "shrinking" year after year.

> If the property or the surrounding neighborhood is not favorable, you don't want the lender to pull the loan a week before it's scheduled closing date because they took a trip out to the site and the property wasn't what they thought it was.

Pictures Of The Property

A picture is worth a thousand words. Sometimes, the lender will request pictures of the property and the surrounding area.

Chapter Ten

Why not forward pictures to them before they ask? If the property or the surrounding neighborhood is not favorable, you don't want the lender to pull the loan a week before it's scheduled closing date because they took a trip out to the site and the property wasn't what they thought it was.

That scenario happened to one of my commercial mortgage broker's other clients. If the property is cosmetically challenged, include the pictures with an improvement plan. Highlight the fact that you are purchasing the property at such a great price due to the property's *cosmetic* situation. Always take whatever negative situation exists and twist it into a positive light.

Verification Of Funds To Close

Where is the money located that you will use to close the property? If you are expected to come to the closing table with a $200,000 down payment, the lender will want to verify that you have $200,000 sitting in the bank, ready to go. If you plan on bringing the money in from a different location, you better get it into your bank account so it can be verified by the lender.

How Much Money Do You *Personally* Have In The Deal?

You know, I hate this one. Nothing infuriates me more about the lending process, than when a lender asks me this question. Personally, I don't think it's any of their business to know where my down payment money came from, as long as it's at the title company on the day of closing. I'll finish my little rant here, but seriously, the lender should give me gold stars or a smiley face sticker on my loan application for coming to the table with the least amount of my own money as possible.

However, lenders don't think that way. They want you to have your own "skin" (money) in the deal. Like my blood, sweat, and tears mean nothing. No matter where the money comes from, get it into your bank account for a month prior to closing. It will then be "seasoned" and it's source won't matter.

Bank Statements

If your personal financial statement indicates your income to be $200,000/year, but your bank statements show only $50,000/year of income, then that discrepancy may cause a red flag to go off in the underwriter's head. Make sure to provide a written explanation for any financial discrepancies.

For instance, many people, such as food servers, card dealers, and bartenders earn the majority of their income from tips. If you were to look at their pay stub, it wouldn't reflect their true income. Everyone knows that people in these types of professions earn more than what is reported on their pay stub. Explaining any financial discrepancies gives the lender assurance that you aren't trying to pull a fast one on them.

3. A LETTER OF INTEREST (LOI) IS ISSUED

How the commercial real estate loan process normally works is something like this: You have a commercial property under contract that you need financing for. You call your mortgage broker and then send him all of the necessary paperwork for the loan package. After he hangs up the telephone from talking with you, he will telephone a commercial real estate lender and say something like this; "I have a client purchasing an apartment building in Redding, California. The value of the property is $2,000,000. She needs a 70% LTV loan. Then the lender will say, "Sure, we can do the loan. Let me send you an

LOI." Seriously, that's how much information a lender will have before they send out an LOI to the borrower.

Now, how can the lender say they can fund the loan, when they haven't even looked at the loan package? It's like a doctor trying to diagnose an illness over the telephone. It's just not that simple!

The lender and/or your mortgage broker will want you to sign an LOI before they will proceed forward. *Be very careful of the wording.* **You do not have to sign it, as it is written. If you don't agree with the way it is worded, change it.**

The lender and/or your mortgage broker will want you to sign an LOI before they will proceed forward. *Be very careful of the wording.* You do not have to sign it, as it is written. If you don't agree with the way it is worded, change it. Put your initials by the changes, and only then, sign your name.

Only when the LOI is signed by the borrower, will the lender review the actual loan package that was submitted from your mortgage broker. **AN LOI MEANS NOTHING!** When the LOI comes from the mortgage broker instead of from the direct lender, it means even less. I don't know if that's technically possible, but you get my point.

4. A COMMITMENT LETTER/TERM SHEET IS ISSUED

After performing a preliminary underwriting review, the lender will issue a commitment letter or term sheet based upon certain conditions being met. The term sheet should provide the details of the exact terms of the loan with such things as lender points, broker points, interest rate, prepayment penalty, and any lock out period, included. When a commitment letter is issued it means that the lender has performed enough due diligence up to that point, that they will *probably* fund the deal.

Something can come up in the appraisal or towards the end of the underwriting process that could change the loan terms, or kill the loan altogether.

The commitment letter is a bit more concrete than an LOI, but funding is far from guaranteed. Something can come up in the appraisal or towards the end of the underwriting process that could change the loan terms, or kill the loan all together.

This happened to me with the Windham, Ohio property. The lender reduced the loan amount offered because the appraisal indicated the property was located in a rural area. I thought that kind of thing should have been caught in underwriting, prior to the appraisal being ordered. It wasn't. You can not count on the loan funding, until you are at the closing table.

Once you sign the lender's commitment letter, the lender will earn their points, which will be paid at closing. This is important to know because if you sign a commitment letter and fail to close the loan on your end, you will still be responsible to pay the broker and lender their points earned. The lender could literally put a lien on the property if you use another lender to purchase the property and refuse to pay the points they earned. Therefore, be sure that when the commitment letter is issued and you sign it, you will be closing the loan with that particular lender. Otherwise, it can be quite an expensive mistake.

Equity Participation

As a condition of the loan approval, the lender may request that they be given an equity position in the property, *in addition to*, the points and interest you will pay for the loan. This is called *equity participation*. I'm adamantly against this. How I view it is, the lender must believe the property will perform well, or they wouldn't want to get in on the action. There are billions of dollars in the world waiting to be lent out. A loan that includes lender equity participation should be used only as a last resort.

> How I view it is, the lender must believe the property will perform well, or they wouldn't want to get in on the action.

5. THE APPRAISAL AND INSPECTIONS ARE ORDERED

Commercial Real Estate Appraisals

Commercial real estate appraisals are way different than residential real estate appraisals. While a residential real estate appraisal costs between $300-$500 and takes about two to three days to complete, a commercial real estate appraisal can cost between $3,000-$8,000, and takes about two to six weeks to complete. There are a lot more factors for the commercial real estate appraiser to take into account. The lender generally orders the appraisal directly from their list of MAI (Member of the Appraisal Institute) certified appraisers.

The appraisal fee is okay to pay up-front, but pay the fee directly to the appraiser. You want to ensure that the money is going to the appraiser and not to the mortgage broker, who says it's going to the appraiser. Ask me how I learned that one!

Survey

Most commercial real estate lenders require a survey of the property to be performed. Like the appraisal, the survey is ordered directly by the lender. A survey verifies where the property boundary lines are. The survey helps provide assurance to the lender that there's nothing located on the property which shouldn't be there (like a neighbor's fence) and that you are indeed purchasing the property you are in contract to purchase.

> The appraisal fee is okay to pay up-front, but pay the fee directly to the appraiser. You want to ensure that the money is going to the appraiser and not to the mortgage broker, who says it's going to the appraiser.

Environmental Reports

The lender may require an environmental report to be performed to ensure that there are no environmental issues that must be dealt with. For instance, if you are purchasing a gas station, then the lender will need to make sure there are no gas or oil leaks contaminating the ground. An environmental report protects not only the lender, but you too!

6. PROVIDE ADDITIONAL ITEMS THE LENDER MAY REQUIRE

Hazard Insurance

You will need to place an insurance policy on the property because the lender won't fund the loan without it. The lender may also dictate the minimum deductible level you must have and the level of coverage you must carry on the policy. The lender may require that you prepay a full year's worth of insurance premiums. That can be a big chunk of money. That happened to me and I wasn't financially prepared for it. Thank goodness the insurance company accepted credit cards.

After the loan closed, I increased the deductible and switched to monthly payments. I personally like a larger deductible so I can afford a higher insurance coverage level. Would you file a claim for something like a $1,000 water leak anyway? No way! I usually choose a $2,000 deductible and then double my insurance coverage. It's really affordable that way.

Make sure to include *Loss of Income Coverage* in your insurance policy. If your property burns down to the ground, the building may be replaced, but it would take time to rebuild. In the meantime, your mortgage payment would still be due each and every month. You will need to make sure that you are covered for the loss of rental income during that time. You can't afford not to have this provision as part of your insurance policy.

Preliminary Title Report

The lender will use a preliminary title report to find the existing encumbrances on the property and to verify that the seller is the legal owner of the property. There may be some interesting things found on the preliminary title report that may negatively impact the property, such as the fact that it's "land locked" meaning there's no legal access to the property. Unknown easements which may have negative implications could be discovered on the preliminary title report as well.

7. CLOSING

There *will* come a day when you finally close on the property. We will go into great detail of the closing process in Chapter 12. While there are many items that you will have to watch out for when working with commercial real estate lenders, the fact is, there will come a time when you will need to apply for a commercial real estate loan. With the information presented here, you will be able to go into the process fully aware of the various things that can prove financially harmful and avoid them at all costs.

SELLER FINANCING

Seller financing makes acquiring commercial real estate so much easier than jumping through a conventional commercial real estate lender's hoops. There are so many benefits of purchasing property with seller financing, that you will be searching high and low for sellers who will "carry paper." These benefits include:

1. Your Closing Costs Will Be Less
2. The Transaction Can Close Faster
3. The Loan Terms Are Often More Favorable Than The Terms Offered By A Commercial Real Estate Lender
4. There Are No LTV Barriers

5. Nobody Questions The Source Of Your Down Payment
6. The Seller Probably Won't Ask About Your Credit Score

Let's examine all of these seller financing benefits in detail.

1. YOUR CLOSING COSTS WILL BE LESS

Let's take a look at the expenses you could save on, by utilizing seller financing.

Appraisal

If you have analyzed the property's numbers and they make sense, why do you need to pay someone to tell you what the property is worth? You just saved yourself $3,000-$8,000.

Mortgage Broker And Lender Fees

You will not be utilizing the services of a commercial mortgage broker or lender, so you will not have to pay their associated costs. For illustrative purposes, let's say on a $2,000,000 loan, that the broker and the lender each charged two points, for a total of four points. The cost would have been $80,000. That's $80,000 in fees you would have paid, on top of the property's purchase price, which you could put toward's the purchase of another commercial property.

Survey

Sometimes you may want to pay for a survey. However, if you view the preliminary title report, and it shows the property lines clearly on the vicinity map, then I would forgo this expense. However, if you are purchasing real estate located in a heavily wooded area, you may want to pay the price and have a survey performed. It really depends upon the situation. If you don't know whether you should have a survey performed or not, error on the side of caution and have it done.

Environmental Reports

Should you pay for an environmental report? Once again, it just depends upon the property. If you are purchasing an apartment building that has always been an apartment building, then you are probably okay to skip an environmental report. However, if you are purchasing a warehouse with the intention of converting it to residential condominiums, I would not skimp out on it. It would just be too risky. You don't know what kind of potentially hazardous materials were used on the site in the past. If the seller doesn't have a recent environmental report, then the expense of having the report done, will have to be negotiated.

Calculating the savings by utilizing seller financing, can be eye opening. In this example, you would have saved a *minimum* of $83,000, on a $2,000,000 loan.

2. THE TRANSACTION CAN CLOSE FASTER

The property can close as quickly as you can complete your due diligence. There's no waiting for such things as the approval from a commercial real estate lender or for an appraisal to be completed.

3. THE LOAN TERMS ARE OFTEN MORE FAVORABLE THAN THE TERMS OFFERED BY A COMMERCIAL REAL ESTATE LENDER

There may be times when the seller just wants to get rid of his property. While you may be thrilled to get a 7% or 8% interest rate, the seller will probably be just as happy as you are to be receiving such a fantastic rate of return to fund his retirement. Most sellers know they will not be able to get a return that high on their money with it sitting in the bank. If the seller is desperate to sell, you can even negotiate an interest rate far below the market interest rate as a requirement of purchasing the property.

4. THERE ARE NO LTV BARRIERS

There are no LTV rules or guidelines with seller financing, like there are with commercial real estate lenders. If the seller is willing to carry a 100% LTV loan, there's nobody that is going to say "no." The only barrier to what LTV the seller is willing to finance is how well you can negotiate the deal.

5. NOBODY QUESTIONS THE SOURCE OF YOUR DOWN PAYMENT

Sellers rarely care where your down payment money comes from. All they care about, is selling their property and getting paid. You will not have to cover your bases in that regard, as long as the money is sent to the title company on the day of closing.

6. THE SELLER PROBABLY WON'T ASK ABOUT YOUR CREDIT SCORE

The seller may ask for your credit report, but most of the time, he won't. The seller knows how the property operates. If the seller is willing to carry a mortgage, that means he has the confidence in the ability of the property to generate enough income to pay the mortgage payment. Seller financing is a great way to start investing in commercial real estate if your credit score is *obscenely* low.

THE NEGATIVE ASPECT OF SELLER FINANCING

The only negative aspect of seller financing I can think of, is that you won't have anyone double checking the property's financials. However, if you have educated yourself, and really combed through the property's financials to verify the information reported by the seller, you should be just fine.

OTHER FINANCING OPTIONS

There are many, many commercial real estate loan programs available to purchase commercial real estate. It would be impossible for me to cover all of them. That's another reason to work with a commercial mortgage broker. Let's go over some alternative commercial real estate financing options you may want to pursue.

1. Hard Money Lenders

If you are having trouble obtaining a conventional commercial real estate loan, you may try applying for a loan with a hard money lender. It's called hard money because the points and the interest rate charged by these lenders are significantly higher than the points and interest rate charged by conventional commercial real estate lenders.

Depending upon the situation, it may be worth the extra cost though. For instance, if you were only going to hold the property for six months, the interest rate shouldn't be a major concern, as long as you can cover the monthly mortgage payment during the short term. The number of points the hard money lender charges would be the more significant factor.

Hard money loans are supposed to be an easier and quicker process, but I personally haven't found that to be true.

Financing a commercial property with a hard money loan is supposed to be a quicker and easier process, but I personally haven't found that to be true.

2. Private Investors

There are many wealthy people in the world with money sitting in the bank earning only 3-4% interest, who would love to earn a higher rate of return on their money. If you could offer those individuals a higher return on their money, which is secured by real estate, they just may take you up on it. Realistically though, you will either need to personally know the person or get a solid recommendation from someone else. Most people don't cut large checks to strangers. I discuss working with private investors more in the next chapter.

3. Cash

Most of the time when I purchase commercial real estate, I'm adamant about putting in the least amount of my own money into the deal as possible. But sometimes, there are reasons why you should be willing to fork over cash. For instance, if you are able to purchase the property for a significant discount for closing quickly. You can always obtain a mortgage on the property after you close the deal. You may even be able to pull out extra money doing it this way.

Another reason why you may want to pay cash for a commercial property is if you are buying it at an auction. It doesn't have to be *your* cash. You can participate in an investor's group that pulls their money together to purchase commercial real estate if you so choose.

4. Private Placement Memorandum (PPM)

A *private placement memorandum* (PPM) is a way of raising funds for your business from investors. This process is regulated by the Securities Exchange Commission, so don't try to do this yourself. I've never financed commercial real estate using this method before, but I have looked into it.

How the process works is that an attorney drafts the PPM, which contains the details of the property and what investment return you are offering the investors. Then, you or your attorney submits the PPM to *qualified* investors You can raise money as a debt placement (promissory note) or as an equity position in the property. Try a debt placement first.

There are also companies that will raise the funds for you, for a percentage of the money raised. Their commissions are much cheaper than a commercial real estate lender's fees. You can offer the investors a fantastic rate of return because you will be saving a ton of money in loan fees. Additionally, you will not have to meet the traditional guidelines imposed by commercial lenders. The time frame for raising funds utilizing a PPM will probably be about the same amount of time it takes for a commercial real estate loan to fund. I'm itching to try this method for my next commercial real estate deal.

Is securing financing to purchase commercial real estate a pain in the butt? Yes, it is. But you only have to do it once. Then you will reap the benefits of the property's cash flow day after day, month after month, and year after year. Compare it with having to get up and go to work day after day, month after month. and year after year.

WHAT NOBODY TELLS YOU

1. There's always money available to purchase commercial real estate. It's just a matter of how much it's going to cost you.
2. Working with a reputable commercial mortgage broker is essential if you will be obtaining financing from a conventional commercial real estate lender.
3. Do not pay up-front fees for your commercial real estate loan.
4. Always be cautious when working with commercial mortgage brokers. Many of them are scam artists.
5. Commercial real estate loans are more expensive than residential real estate loans.
6. You can not borrow as high of an LTV on commercial real estate loans, as you can on residential real estate loans.
7. Seller financing is the easiest and cheapest way to finance commercial real estate.

Chapter 11
Got Money?

We've already discussed the fact that when you are purchasing commercial real estate you will need to come up with a lot more money for the down payment than you will when purchasing residential real estate. This is the number one reason why most people do not invest in commercial real estate. However, there are ways around this obstacle. The number of ways of finding money for the down payment is only limited to how creative you can be. Let's go over some of my favorite ways to find those down payment funds.

HOME EQUITY

If you are reading this book, you most likely already own some type of real estate, whether it is your personal home or a residential investment property. It is also more than likely, with the significant appreciation levels which have occurred over the last few years that you are sitting on a large amount of equity in that property which can be used as your own mini bank fund.

Utilizing the equity in my home is how I purchased my first commercial property. I refinanced my home and pulled out $200,000. Then I started my search for a commercial property to purchase. What made my situation particularly beneficial was the fact that I never paid any money out of my pocket when I initially purchased my home. I utilized an "80/20" loan (80% first mortgage coupled with a 20% second mortgage) and the seller paid all of the closing costs. I used my property, which cost me nothing out of my own pocket to purchase, as my personal bank fund to build my wealth. You too, can utilize the equity of a property you own to build your own commercial real estate empire.

WHY YOU SHOULD USE THE EQUITY IN YOUR HOME TO PURCHASE COMMERCIAL REAL ESTATE

There are four primary reasons why using your home equity to come up with the down payment to purchase commercial real estate is a financially smart move. Let's go over them.

Leaving Large Amounts Of Equity In A Property Is Like Begging To Be Sued

Let's say that someone slips and falls on a property you own. That person consults with an attorney with plans to sue you for $200,000 for "pain and suffering." Since most people don't have the financial ability to pay the typical $200-$300 hourly fee that attorneys charge, the attorney will usually work on a contingency basis. Simply put, the attorney is paid only if there is a settlement reached or a favorable verdict for the plaintiff.

One of the primary factors of whether an attorney will accept a contingency case or not, is the financial strength of the proposed defendant. Do you think it's likely that an attorney will take on a contingency case against a proposed defendant who has $300,000 of equity in their home? Absolutely! What if the proposed defendant only has $20,000 of equity in their home? Is it likely that the attorney would take the case on then? Probably not.

Do you think it's likely that an attorney will take on a contingency case against a proposed defendant who has $300,000 of equity in their home? Absolutely! What if the proposed defendant only has $20,000 of equity in their home? Is it likely that the attorney would take the case on then? Probably not.

Leaving Large Levels Of Equity In Your Home Protects The Bank, Not You

Most people were raised to believe that a substantial amount of home equity financially protects you against unfortunate situations, such as an unforseen job loss. However, that's not how I view it at all. In the unfortunate circumstance that the property is foreclosed upon, any equity in the property becomes the bank's equity. The larger the amount of equity in the property, the safer your lender's loan is in the event you default on the loan. It doesn't protect you.

Chapter Eleven

Use It Or Lose It?

Here's another thought-think about all of those people in the New Orleans area who lost their homes in Hurricane Katrina. Almost everyone who had equity in their home lost their equity with it. "That's what insurance is for." you may say. But, even with the proper type of insurance coverage, which a vast majority of the homeowners didn't have, negotiating a fair insurance settlement with an insurance company is nearly impossible. However, if the homeowners would have utilized their home equity to purchase investment real estate, they would not have lost their home equity, unless all of their investment properties were located in the same localized area.

It's A Fantastic Way To Leverage Your Way To Wealth

Banks borrow money from the Federal Reserve or from their customers and then lend it out for a higher interest rate than they paid to borrow it. Why not take advantage of this strategy as well by utilizing your home equity? It obviously works! It's a proven strategy which you may want to think about. You too can leverage other people's money to build your wealth.

You Will Decrease Your Tax Obligation By Increasing The Amount Of Mortgage Interest You Pay

By extracting the equity out of a property to use it as a down payment to purchase commercial real estate, you will create a situation where you will be paying on three loans instead of one. Don't let that freak you out. Mortgage debt is a good thing! The cash flow that will you receive from the commercial property you purchase should cover the monthly mortgage payment for both the home equity loan on your residential property and the first mortgage on your commercial property. Don't purchase the commercial property if it doesn't. The mortgage interest you pay on all three loans is a tax deductible expense. This will create a favorable tax situation for you.

I only recommend extracting the equity from a property for those people who will use the money to purchase investment real estate. I do not recommend that anyone should utilize a property's equity to purchase an automobile, take a vacation, or go shopping.

CREDIT CARDS

I love, love, love using credit cards to fund the down payment to purchase real estate. However, you will find that when you are purchasing commercial real estate, that your credit card line will probably not be high enough to fund the entire down payment amount. However, it may be large enough to cover the earnest deposit, which enables you to tie the property up with a purchase contract. You would then have the time to bring together money investors to complete the deal.

Business Credit Card Lines Are Usually Higher Than Personal Credit Cards Lines

What I have found is that once you have a business established, it is significantly easier to acquire business credit cards than it is to acquire personal credit cards. The credit lines are usually larger as well.

Once again, if you don't have financial self control, I don't advise that you seek out numerous high limit credit card lines. If you don't have self control then you may want to think twice about purchasing commercial real estate anyway, as commercial real estate ownership requires a high money management skill level.

RETIREMENT ACCOUNTS

Find People Who Have Money Sitting In A Low Interest Earning Retirement Account

There are billions of dollars sitting in many different types of retirement accounts, such as an IRA or a 401K. Most people don't want to think about their investment options, so when they leave their job they'll usually just keep their retirement account within their former employer's plan. This is not the most favorable situation because the investment choices within those types of plans are extremely limited.

A more favorable option is to roll the retirement plan into a self directed IRA. A self directed IRA is a retirement plan which doesn't limit your investment choices to only stocks, bonds, and mutual funds. With a self directed IRA your investment choices may include investing in such things as promissory notes, real estate, mortgages, equipment leases, and more. The vast number of investment choices that a self directed IRA allows is what makes this retirement plan such a fantastic choice, which most people aren't aware even exists.

The key to finding money for the down payment to purchase commercial real estate is finding those people who have money sitting in a retirement account with a former employer

and then educating them about the choices of investing with you through a self directed IRA. Let them know how you can offer them a much higher investment rate
of return than they are currently receiving through their employer's plan. It's not difficult to do.

For more information about self directed IRA's visit www.trustetc.com.

Borrow Money Against Your 401K

If you are currently employed and have a 401K retirement account, you can borrow money from it. The interest you pay on the loan will be paid back to your 401K account, which just increases your wealth even more.

SELL OTHER REAL ESTATE YOU OWN

Just like in the game of Monopoly, sometimes it's a wise financial move to sell smaller investment properties to step up to larger investment properties. That is what I did with my condo. It had appreciated quite a bit. When I couldn't pull out as much money as I wanted through a cash-out refinance, I opted to sell it.

I was able to leverage the $70,000 profit into the condo conversion property, which when completed, should bring me a $1,000,000 profit. Without the $70,000 from the sale of my condo, I wouldn't have had enough money to purchase the condo conversion property. Consistently evaluate your current real estate holdings to determine if you should hold onto them or if you should leverage the equity into larger properties.

Chapter Eleven

PRIVATE INVESTORS

There are many people who would like to take advantage of the higher rate of return that real estate investments can offer, but they don't want to spend the time learning how to properly analyze real estate deals to make it happen. It takes a lot of education and real-life experience to properly learn how to make wise real estate investment decisions.

> The fact is, no matter how great the proposed return on investment may be, if you do not have a high level of integrity, nobody is going to open up their pocketbook for you.

When you are successful with residential real estate investments, people will wonder how you did it. These are the people who you should ask to invest with you in your next real estate deal.

Finding Money Investors Is Not Easy

You will find several real estate investing books where the author tells you that finding money investors is easy. I will be the one author who tells you it's not. Many people may express an interest in investing with you, however when it comes down to actually cutting you a check, it's a whole different story.

Realistically, you will need to ask people who you personally know to invest with you. Most people will not cut a check to a stranger unless you have come highly recommended by someone else.

Money Investors Are Investing On You, As A Person

When a money investor hands over a check to you, what they are saying is that they trust you as a person and in the knowledge you have. The fact is, no matter how great the proposed return on investment may be, if you do not have a high level of integrity, nobody is going to open up their pocketbook for you. When they do, it's a tremendous compliment *and* also a tremendous responsibility.

All of my money investors have been people who I personally know. When your money investors are people you personally know, it makes you choose your real estate investments even more carefully than usual, as your decisions impact not only your financial future, but their financial future as well.

Start By Asking For Small Amounts Of Money

I wouldn't suggest that you ask a money investor for a large amount of money, such as $100,000 on your first deal together. It can happen, but it's a bit unrealistic. Instead, ask them to invest smaller amounts of money such as $1,000, $5,000, or $10,000. Doing deals with smaller amounts of money gives the money investor time to gain confidence in you.

You only need to convince a money investor to invest with you once. Once you return their money from your first deal together, the first thing they want to know is, "When's the next deal coming?"

Chapter Eleven

Find People Who Know Potential Money Investors

Sometimes a person will be interested in investing with you, but they personally lack the financial resources to do so. However, they may still have the opportunity to make some money from the deal. If they know someone who does have money to invest, they may act as a money finder or a middleman. For instance, if I was offering a 30% rate of return and they could find an investor who is willing to accept a 20% rate of return, then the middleman would receive the 10% rate of return difference, without investing any of his own money.

STRUCTURING THE DEAL WITH YOUR MONEY INVESTORS

There is No "Right" Way To Structure Investment Agreements

There are many different ways you can structure the actual investment agreement with your money investors. It boils down to whatever works for the two parties involved in the deal. Once you have the basic agreement in mind, you or an attorney can draft the agreement.

The most important thing about the agreement, is to make sure it is in writing. Outlining all aspects of the deal insures that your money investors know that you are a serious business person and that the contract is legally binding. If written properly, the contact makes all terms and conditions of the agreement crystal clear for all parties involved. Your money investors must understand the possible risks involved with the investment and any potential for delay in payment.

Retain All Of The Control

I like being in complete control of the investment decisions because I know how much time I have spent educating myself, as well as my motivation level. I structure my investment agreements so that the money investors are passive. They have no control over the property decisions. They are, after all, banking on my expertise and experience. However, this type of arrangement may not work for you. You may be the type of person who likes to bounce ideas off your money investors before making investment decisions.

You can also have a democratic situation where everyone gets a vote. If you choose to give your money investors a voice in the direction of the investment, be aware that it may present a problem down the road if the group cannot reach a unanimous decision.

Secured Or Unsecured?

I usually sign an unsecured promissory note with my money investors. Your money investors may be hesitant about not having their note secured by the property. For some reason, most people feel it is safe to

> For some reason, most people feel it is safe to invest in the stock market, which is an unsecured investment. Yet when it comes to placing an investment with an individual, utilizing an unsecured promissory note, somehow it's "risky."

invest in the stock market, which is an unsecured investment. Yet when it comes to placing an investment with an individual, utilizing an unsecured promissory note, somehow it's "risky."

Either the investor believes in you and the project or they don't. The reason the investment needs to be arranged in this manner is to ensure that the lender thinks the entire down payment came solely from you. As I mentioned before, I don't believe the source of the down payment is any of the lender's business. If the promissory note is to be secured against the property, make sure it's recorded after the property closes.

Keep Everything Separate

You should keep all of the property's paperwork and it's financial records separate from your personal or other business records and accounts. A separate checking account, used exclusively for the property, should be opened so that the property's funds are not commingled with your other investments. A proper corporate structure should be established as well, with the help of your financial advisors.

Collect The Money From The Money Investors And Then Cut One Check To The Title Company

Deposit the funds from your money investors into the established bank account (which impresses your bank) and then cut one check or wire transfer the money to the title company.

On the condo conversion project, I had two of my investors send the money directly to the title company instead of to me.

The title company saw that the money had not come directly from me and made my investors sign a piece acknowledging the money would be returned to me, not to them, in the event the property did not close.

Additionally, the closing statement (HUD-1) showed how much of the down payment money came from these people. If you want to refinance the mortgage in the future this can present a problem as the, "How much money do you personally have in the deal?" question may come up.

Long story short, there is no benefit of having your money investors send the money to the title company instead of giving it to you, while there can be many potential problems caused from it.

Make The Note Assignable To A Different Project

There will be times when the property you have raised money for will not close. Make sure you have not obligated yourself to pay your money investors interest unless the property does close. You may also want to make the note assignable to a different property, if it is acceptable for both parties.

Raise Enough Money To Pay Yourself

There's nothing worse than being property rich and cash poor. The time frame for finding a property to purchase, finding money investors, performing the due diligence, obtaining financing, and closing the deal takes a lot longer with commercial real estate than it does with residential real estate. In the meantime, your mortgage payment and other living expenses have to be paid. You must raise enough money to cover your monthly expenses for the anticipated time frame it will take you to go through the purchasing process because if you don't, it is extremely stressful.

For instance, I thought it would take a *maximum* of one year to complete the condo conversion project. It will be closer to two years. After I maxed out all of my credit cards to close the property, I barely had enough money to live off of. It's not a good way to live and I won't put myself in that situation again, nor should you.

KEEP THE LINES OF COMMUNICATION WITH YOUR MONEY INVESTORS OPEN

Just like life, investments don't always go as planned. I'm in that situation right now with the condo conversion project. My money investors were told that the investment would take no longer than a year. However, it's been 21 months so far.

This delay has caused a couple of my money investors into a tight financial situation. While my money investors continue to accrue interest until their investment is paid in full, it just kills me to know that I was not able to fulfill my obligation when I said I would.

To ensure that my investors are consistently aware of the progress of the development, I send them an email every one to two weeks. I want to keep them informed about how hard I am working to get things done as quickly as possible. I never want anyone to feel sorry about investing with me.

I hope you were able to get a couple of ideas of how you can raise money for a down payment to purchase commercial real estate. As I mentioned before, it's really a matter of your creativity and more importantly, your determination.

WHAT NOBODY TELLS YOU

1. Leaving a large amount of equity in your home protects the bank, not you.
2. Finding money investors can be tough, but you only have to convince them once.
3. Money investors only cut checks to people who they trust and believe in, regardless of the strength of the deal.
4. Money sitting in a retirement account (yours or someone else's) is a relatively unutilized down payment source.

CHAPTER 12
THE CLOSING

The big closing day is here. It's time to close the property. Be prepared to get writer's cramp from signing the stack of closing documents that will bring you one step closer to a lifetime of wealth. As you can tell, getting to the closing table has been a much more extensive process than closing any residential property. It may have taken you months or even years to get to this point. But just because you are at the closing table, doesn't mean you should let your guard down. There's still plenty of items you will need to pay close attention to. Let's go over the closing process.

THE TITLE COMPANY OR ATTORNEY WILL TAKE CARE OF EVERYTHING

In certain states, it is customary to close a real estate transaction at an attorney's office. In other states, it is customary to use a title company to close a real estate transaction. I've always closed my real estate transactions with a title company. That is why you will find I always reference the closing with a title company in this book, even though your transaction may close at an attorney's office.

You do not need to be physically present at the place a closing will occur. The closing documents can be sent to you via an overnight courier. You will sign the documents in front of a notary and then send them back to the title company.

CLOSING FEES

The closing fees are broken down on a HUD-1 statement. Because you are purchasing commercial real estate which is generally more expensive than residential real estate, the closing fees will be correspondingly higher.

Check The Accuracy Of The HUD-1 Statement Prior To The Closing Date

Ask the title company for a copy of the HUD-1 statement prior to the closing date. As good as title companies are, they sometimes miss seller credits or unusual provisions written in the purchase contract. It is well known that title companies add unnecessary fees to pad their profit on the closing statement. They know that most people do not ask for their HUD-1 statement prior to closing and even if a client finds something inaccurate they will not hold up the closing to have it corrected. Plus, you don't want to have to focus on the accuracy of the HUD-1 statement on the closing date. Instead you want to be able to focus on the accuracy of the mortgage documents.

WHAT IS ON A HUD-1 STATEMENT?

1. Lender Fees
These are the points and other fees your lender charges for funding the loan which will show up as an expense.

2. Broker Fees
If you used the services of a commercial mortgage broker, his commission will show up as an expense.

3. Tenant's Security Deposits
The tenant's security deposits will be transferred to you at closing as a credit from the seller.

4. Title Company Fees
You will purchase title insurance from the title company for yourself and for your lender. You will also pay the associated fees of the closing, such as recording fees, notary fees, and payment to the title company for handling the transaction.

5. Prorations
Property tax and hazard insurance will be prorated for a certain number of months per your lender's request.

6. Seller Credits
Any seller credits listed in the purchase agreement should show up as a credit. Make sure they are there!

7. Loan Amount
The loan amount from the lender should be indicated as a credit. If there are two lenders (first and second mortgage holders) both loan amounts should be indicated.

READ THE MORTGAGE DOCUMENTS IN DETAIL PRIOR TO SIGNING THE PAPERWORK

The first commercial property I purchased was a 57 unit apartment complex in Windham, Ohio. I was so excited when the package containing the closing documents arrived. I had worked on the deal for seven months and I was anxious to finally get the transaction closed. I briefly scanned the paperwork, particularly the interest rate. Everything seemed to be in order.

We were on a strict time line, as the closing documents had to be back to the title company by the next day for the title to record on the last day of the month. We found a DHL drop box which indicated the pick up time was at 3:00 PM. I had arrived at 2:45 PM. I dropped the package in and waited until 3:15 PM-still no DHL truck arrived. It must be late, I thought before I left.

The next day I received a telephone call from the title company. They hadn't received the paperwork. Confused by this, I said, "I don't understand. It should be there. I will call DHL and find out what's going on." After talking to a representative, I found out that the truck had come early that day, at 2:30 PM to be exact. The closing documents wouldn't arrive at the title company until the next day. That messed everything up, as it would be a new month, and the mortgage documents would have to be redrawn.

I couldn't believe that I had worked so hard on this deal and things just kept going wrong! The lender agreed to redraw the mortgage documents, but they wanted $2,000 to do so. My mortgage broker convinced the lender to waive the fee. When the revised mortgage documents arrived, I was so anxious to get them back to the title company so the deal could finally close, that I didn't bother to ensure that the lender's term in the mortgage documents matched what was agreed upon. Big mistake!!!

After the property closed, I discovered the lock out period had been changed from a two year term to a four year term. I would have never agreed to a four year lock out because the second mortgage had a balloon payment due in three years. I would have to refinance the loan

When the lender was informed of this, they merely blew me off saying, "You signed the note." Damn it! I hate when they're right.

to pay it off before then. When the lender was informed of this, they merely blew me off saying, "You signed the note." Damn it! I hate when they're right.

I don't know if the lender changed the lock out period intentionally or not. Either way, it was my fault for neglecting to make sure that all the terms in the mortgage documents were correct.

Lenders pull this kind of stuff because they know that most people will not send incorrect paperwork back. Go to my website, www.monicavillasenor.net, to see a copy of the lender's conditional loan approval letter which indicates a two year lock out term. You can compare it to the provision in the note which shows that the lock out term was changed to four years.

What's the moral of the story? Read EVERYTHING in the

mortgage documents. Is the interest rate, prepayment penalty, lock out period, and amortization schedule correct? If not, don't be afraid of delaying the closing and sending the paperwork back.

WHAT NOBODY TELLS YOU

1. Make sure the HUD-1 statement is correct by reviewing it prior to the closing date.
2. Lenders change terms in the mortgage note without your knowledge. If you don't catch the changes, then you will be stuck with them.

CHAPTER 13
YOU OWN IT.
NOW WHAT?

It's quite a strange feeling to go through the entire process of purchasing a commercial property only to realize there's still a bit of transition to go. We are about to discuss bookkeeping and property management. Try to line up these people prior to closing on the property if possible so the transition can go smoother.

HIRE A BOOKKEEPER

Prior to the purchase of your first commercial property, you may not have had the need for the services of a bookkeeper. That was certainly the case for me. When my first commercial property finally closed, I had to find a bookkeeper-and fast! I placed an ad in the newspaper. After several interviews, I found Cheryl seemed to be the right fit for me. Cheryl is an outgoing mother of two boys, who was seeking a position where she could work from home. I related to that, as I also work from home and have two boys of my own. She also had construction experience. But, most importantly, I trusted my gut. You must find someone who is trustworthy, as they will have access to all of your financial information.

Don't Waste Your Time Doing Your Own Books

You may be thinking you could save yourself money by doing your own bookkeeping. Wrong, wrong, wrong. Hiring a bookkeeper is something I consider not optional. You are a real estate investor, not a bookkeeper. Bookkeepers are experts in their field. They can complete a financial task in two hours what would take you five hours to complete. You can't get time back. You should not be spending hours inputting income and expenses, auditing your bank records, and sending out invoices.

The whole point of leveraging into commercial real estate is to become financially free. I think it's a pretty safe assumption to say that most people don't want to spend their free time organizing their property's financials. You can expand your business and grow your wealth faster by handing over certain tasks to people who are experts in their field.

I really cannot emphasize enough how much a bookkeeper will help you. Just add the cost of hiring a bookkeeper as a fixed expense of the property when analyzing a commercial property.

Hire Your Bookkeeper From The Beginning

The property management company I hired for the condo conversion property provided me with a monthly income and expense report, so I didn't think I needed the services of my bookkeeper for that property. However, nobody was auditing what was being paid by the property management company. I certainly didn't have the time to make sure that the property management company was paying everything correctly. Don't be naive in thinking that your property management company will always get your financial reports right. My bookkeeper was spending so much time on the telephone with the property management company asking questions about their financial reports that it was actually costing me more money than if she did them herself.

You Will Learn A Lot

My bookkeeper, Cheryl, has taught me quite a few things that I would not have thought of, which has helped the operation of the property run smoother. For instance, she told me to take a copy of each rental check, so I could refer back to it at any time. All of the copies of the rental checks in a deposit are then stapled to the deposit slip, so you can tell which checks comprise that particular deposit.

I can't tell you how many times being able to refer back to the copy of a rental check has proved useful. Just the other day, my bank's proof department deducted $150.00 from a deposit. Cheryl called me and said, "You need to call the bank to find out why they are deducting $150.00 from this deposit because everything looks like it adds up." I referred back to the deposit which had all of the copies of the rental checks attached. It seems that the bank had credited a $81.00 money order, as a $31.00 money order. That accounted for $50.00. I also found a check that I thought was written for $127.00, was actually written for $27.00. That accounted for the other $100.00. If I hadn't had a copy of those checks, I would not have been able to figure out the problem so easily.

Chapter Thirteen

Your Taxes Will Be So Much Easier

If you have not been keeping up with on your books at the end of the year you really have two options. They are:

1. Try to figure out everything yourself and get completely stressed out.
2. Give your CPA a big bunch of papers and say, "Figure it out."

Either way, it will cost you. One way costs you in time and stress. The other way costs you in money. Spend the money on a bookkeeper, so you will save both time and money.

I have been extremely fortunate to find such a wonderful person as my bookkeeper, who not only does a great job, but who I consider a friend. Working together has been eye opening for her as well. She has had a front row seat in my investment projects. She has seen how it's been a ton of work and how I have chosen to handle the obstacles along the way. Hopefully, you too will find a bookkeeper who works with you as well as Cheryl and I work together.

PROPERTY MANAGEMENT

Boy, do I have some stories for you here. I couldn't make up some of the experiences I've had during the course of owning 81 apartment units. There's a vast difference between managing apartment buildings versus managing over types of commercial real estate. Because of this, I have broken each section into it's appropriate area.

APARTMENTS

WHO DO YOU HIRE?

You will have two main options when choosing who to hire to manage your commercial real estate. You can choose to hire a property manager directly or you can choose to hire a property management company. Let's discuss both options in further detail.

Hire A Property Manager Directly

I usually choose to hire a property manager directly if possible. Although that option would probably be an unrealistic choice for those apartment complexes containing over 100 units.

Before we closed on the property in Windham, Ohio I had the intention of hiring the seller to manage the property, as she owned a property management company. However, during the property inspection the seller left and had a lady named Lesley take over. As we went from unit to unit, Lesley knew all the tenant's names and spoke in depth to each one. I was completely impressed. It was obvious that she was the one who was making the day to day contact with the tenants, not the seller. By the end of the day, it was apparent that it wasn't the property management company I needed to hire, rather it was Lesley I needed to hire.

What finalized my decision to hire Lesley directly was when I received a property management proposal from the seller. She wanted a 15% property management fee. I knew the customary property management fee was 5-10% of the rental income collected. The seller must have thought I just fell off

221

a turnip truck. She wasn't even doing the work, Lesley was. As the closing date drew near, I called Lesley at the office and presented her with the idea of working for me directly.

She was ecstatic about the idea. Come to find out, Lesley couldn't stand working for the seller anymore. In fact, she had already given the seller a two week notice. The arrangement we worked out allowed Lesley to receive a significant pay increase, while I would save the expense of the middleman.

The seller was unpleasantly surprised to find out that not only was she not going to be getting my business, but I had "stole" her employee as well. The arrangement worked out well for all parties (except for the seller). I am happy to say that Lesley and her husband have been able to get ahead financially and have already started experiencing their own real estate investing success.

Hire A Property Management Company

Property management companies are the middleman I was referencing above. They just hire people to do the work for them, so the company is only as good as the people they hire. Your property will probably not be the only one they manage, so their focus will not be exclusively on taking care of your property. They are also not going to be concerned with your financial bottom line as you are because they are paid a commission based off of the property's gross rental income collected, rather than on the property's net income.

THE DISADVANTAGES OF HIRING A PROPERTY MANAGEMENT COMPANY

You May Not Know What's Going On With Your Property

Hiring a property management company is a double edge sword. On one hand, they shield you from the day to day crap that comes with managing tenants. On the other hand, there may be situations that need addressed, which you would never know about because they won't report it to you.

> Hiring a property management company is a double edge sword. On one hand, they shield you from the day to day crap that comes with managing tenants. On the other hand, there may be situations that need addressed, which you would never know about because they won't report it to you.

This situation happened to me with the condo conversion property in Redding, California. I hired a property management company owned by a gentleman named Frank (fictitious name). What initially drew me to hiring Frank was the fact that he was a straight forward, to the point, type of guy. I felt he would get things done.

As the months went by, I started receiving reports from my resident manager regarding certain situations I felt should have been reported to me, which weren't. When I called Frank to discuss it, Frank yelled at me, "You hired me to manage your property. Let me manage it or fire me!" I was

223

stunned. I just couldn't believe that he would talk to me, the property owner like that. I would have fired him right then and there, but I was afraid he would do something vindictive to sabotage the condo conversion. I decided it wouldn't be wise to gamble on his behavior until after I received the condo conversion approval from the city officials. Then I could fire him.

However, the condo conversion approval took a lot longer than anticipated. A couple more months passed by when I received another telephone call, this time from a tenant. I don't usually give my telephone number to my tenants. However, due to the condo conversion, I wanted them to be able to contact me as needed with any questions or concerns they had. The tenant informed me of the fact that Frank was treating him and his wife rudely. He told me, that he was not the only one either, that many of my other tenants were unhappy with Frank's consistently brash behavior. I knew where the tenant was coming from, as I had personally experienced that type of behavior from Frank.

I told the tenant to get everyone's complaints about Frank in writing. If as many tenants were unhappy as he reported, then I would fire him. I had seven (out of 24 units) written complaints faxed to me the next day. The tenants had thought I knew about Frank's continual rude behavior directed towards them. They were scared to talk to the guy. I had no choice. I had to let him go and just pray that he would not do something that would ruin the condo conversion.

Upon receiving the termination letter, although genuinely surprised, Frank didn't display any vindictive behavior.

The point of this story is to help you understand how you may be left out of the loop regarding your property when you hire a property management company. You won't know the whole story of what's going on with the property. This actually might be your ideal situation. For me, it's not. While I don't like to take on the day to day property operations, I'm just too much of a control freak to be left completely in the dark about what's going on. It is just good business sense to check in on your property to make sure things are getting done in a way that YOU, the property owner, want things done.

They Won't Watch Your Bottom Line

Since the property management company's fee comes from a percentage of the gross income collected, not the net income, they don't do everything possible to save you money. For instance, Frank once hired a painting contractor to paint one of the vacant units, at a cost of $2,000. I almost passed out! In Ohio, I can get the interior of a comparably sized unit painted for about $500. Both contractors were making money, however one contractor was making way more profit than he should have. It made me wonder if there wasn't some kind of kick back going on between the painting contractor and Frank.

THE PROPERTY MANAGEMENT CONTRACT

Make The Agreement As Specific As Possible

The property management agreement must be written with all terms and conditions spelled out in detail. Pay specific attention to the property management fee charged, the length of the contract, and any special fees they may assess. You want to make sure that there's an escape out of any property management contract you sign. If you can negotiate a month to month property management agreement, that is best. You don't want to be stuck paying a property management company who sucks (yes, that is a technical word).

How Are Property Managers Paid?

Typical property management fees run from 5-10% of the rental income collected. If you are receiving quotes above this range, you should know it's out of line. Pay close attention to how the contract is written. Is the property management fee based upon the rental income collected or is it based upon the property's gross income collected? The difference is significant.

Some property management companies will want the contract written in a way that allows them to keep late fees assessed to the tenants. Don't go for this. They should not get a bonus for collecting rental income late. They should also not be paid a commission on any late fees.

You can also work out an arrangement where the property management company is paid per occupied unit. For instance a $20/occupied unit property management fee for a 50 unit apartment complex, would be a $1,000 monthly fee (assuming a 100% occupancy level).

I like paying the property management fee as a percentage of the rental income collected because it gives the property manager an incentive to keep the property occupied. It also provides a built in raise anytime rental rates are increased. I also give a bonus to the property manger when a vacant unit is filled with a tenant. If your property is just one of many they manage, it gives them a reason to place the tenant in your property first.

Rent Collection Methods

Don't allow your property manger to accept cash. It's just wrought with potential problems. There's no paper trail if there's ever a question of whether or not rent was collected. In additional to the traditional ways a tenant may pay rent, like with a check or money order, I offer my tenants the opportunity of paying their rent by credit card. I haven't had a tenant take advantage of this yet, as most of my tenants don't even own credit cards, but I think it would be a popular payment option in certain areas.

There are also companies that allow a landlord to automatically deduct the rental amount from the tenant's bank account. The more ways you can offer the tenant to pay their rent, the better.

Security Deposits

Make sure your property manager forwards any new tenant's security deposit to you. You want the money sitting in your bank account, earning you interest rather than financially benefitting the property management company.

BE CAREFUL OF THE LAW

Every state has it's own laws which must be complied with in regards to property management and tenant's rights. You must not assume that because something is legal in one state, it is legal in another state. Read each state's statues and regulations to ensure you are complying with the law.

Chapter Thirteen

Property Management Laws

Who can or cannot act as a property manager is regulated by each individual state. For instance, in Ohio, you can self manage your property or you can hire a real estate broker (or their company). Someone can't just wake up one day and say, "I think I'll become a property manager today." It would be illegal. In California, any property with 12 or more dwelling units must have an onsite property manager, in addition to any regular property management company you may choose to hire.

These laws have been put into place to protect not only the tenants, but to also protect property owners against unscrupulous people who have the intent to financially gain at the owner's expense. However, the intent is not always followed. Check out this story-I couldn't make it up if I tried....

In any small town, like Windham, Ohio where I own apartment units, small town politics run rampant. Everyone knows everyone else's business. A complaint was filed with the Ohio Department of Real Estate (DRE) against my property manager, Lesley, alleging she was illegally practicing property management because she is not a real estate broker. The DRE would not tell us who filed the complaint, however, the documentation they had made it clear it was filed by the owner of the only property management company is town. This person also happens to be a member of the city council.

The DRE launched a formal investigation against Lesley, even after I explained to them that I self manage the property and that Lesley works directly underneath me. She has no authority to make property management decisions. The DRE

228

asked me for certain paperwork, which I refused to give them without a subpoena, because I considered the information confidential. They took me up on my offer. It was one of those situations that was so moronic, I couldn't believe it had seriously gotten to that point. I decided I better protect Lesley with a job description specifically pointing out that she has no decision making capacity regarding the property.

About a month later, the DRE set up a public hearing before the Ohio Real Estate Commission to render a verdict of whether she was "guilty" of illegally practicing property management or not. You would not believe what happened at the meeting, as even I have a hard time believing it and I witnessed it. Go to my website, www.monicavillasenor.net, to get the conclusion to the story (it's a long one).

The complaint that was filed, was not filed to protect the tenants or the property owner. It was filed for selfish and vindictive purposes. Since that happened, the Village of Windham has proposed an ordinance which would make it illegal for any property owner to hire a property management company located outside the Village of Windham. I think it's really sad that the only way a local company can maintain business is by forcing it with a law. You can see that proposed ordinance and my response letter regarding this ordinance on my website as well. I'm sure after reading this book, Lesley will be loved by those folks even more!

Tenant's Rights

Tenants have a lot of rights. I don't think they understand how protected they are. You and your property manager need to understand the requirements of the law pertaining to tenants so you can comply with them. Let an attorney handle any

229

evictions so they have the responsibility of performing the process the correct way.

Whichever way you decide to manage your commercial property, you must find something that works for you. If you don't want to be disturbed at all, then a full property management company may suit you best. If you are more of the hands-on type of person who needs to be involved, then you may be better off hiring an onsite resident manager who can be your eyes and ears, while you stay in control of the management decisions.

HANDLING TENANTS

Don't Be A Slum Lord

After purchasing my property in Ohio, which happens to be occupied by many low income tenants, people would often remark, "So, you're a slum lord now." What a slap in the face! Why? Because nothing pisses me off more than slum lords. While my properties may not be as pretty as some other properties and while my tenants may be lower income, a "slum lord" is a description of the type of person who owns the property, not a description of the property itself. Slum lords

> While my property may not be as pretty as some other properties and while my tenants may be lower income, a "slum lord" is a description of the type of person who owns the property, not a description of the property itself.

are property owners who treat their tenants like crap, which I do not. When a tenant signs a rental agreement with the property owner, as long as the tenant is living up to his obligations under the lease agreement, the landlord must live up to his obligations too. This includes treating the tenant with respect, fixing items in a timely fashion, and providing a safe and clean living environment. I've personally witnessed my share of landlords who come up short in the integrity department and milk the property for every penny.

Don't Let Tenants Perform Their Own Repairs

If you allow a tenant to make their own repairs, you will end up paying for it down the road. Let's say a tenant puts a hole in the wall and you agree to let him fix it himself. When he eventually moves out, you see that the "repair" is a mess. You will have to have someone come out and repair the tenant's "repair." Just call a professional and have it done right the first time. You can always send your tenant an invoice.

You will also be better protected against lawsuits this way. If a repair is made incorrectly, and someone gets hurt as a result of it, you won't have much legal protection. The tenant can also injure themselves while making the repair, which also exposes you to being sued.

Document Everything

Have you ever had any problems with your tenants? No way! Me too! Here's the deal. 90% of tenants are a pleasure to have. It's just those remaining 10% that cause the majority of the problems.

Chapter Thirteen

I had an interesting situation with a former tenant of my condo conversion property. The former tenant had called me to see when I would be returning his security deposit. I normally pay security deposits back quickly, however in his situation I needed more time because I had to get a bid for new carpeting. That was because his unit reeked like a litter box. I told the tenant that I would try to have the carpet professionally cleaned first, but if that didn't remove the smell, then I would have to replace the carpet. After a professional cleaning, the carpet still was unsalvageable.

I informed my former tenant he would not be receiving any of his security deposit back. If I really wanted to be tough, I could have sued him for the $300 difference he should have still owed me. Instead, I was willing to allow him to walk away with no additional money owed. Fuming, he said, "You must have gone into the wrong apartment. I cleaned the carpets and there was no foul smell." I felt he was the type of person who would take me to court. If he decided to do so, I was okay with it. Five people had been in his apartment to film for my reality show and could serve as witnesses if necessary. If I hadn't had witnesses, I would have kept a sample of the carpet and pad as "evidence."

Having witnesses was the documentation I needed to protect myself from a lawsuit in this case. However, most of the time documentation will either be a written letter or a picture. For instance, if you gave a tenant a warning about their dog, it better have been in writing and placed in a folder. If someone complains about another tenant, the complaining tenant should put it in writing.

Judges are usually tough on landlords, so the more proof you can provide to back up your case, such as pictures, letters, or witnesses, the more likely it is that you would receive a favorable verdict.

RETAIL/OFFICE

While I don't personally own any retail buildings, I was in contract to purchase one. I had to research out potential property management companies and how they differed from property management companies that handle apartment buildings.

What I found is that they differ significantly. Those property management companies who handle retail or office buildings have property management companies that handle retail and office properties have much less hands-on work. The tenants do not have an, "I am entitled" attitude, like many tenants have in apartment buildings. They are business owners who care about the property because the success of their business relies upon it. As the property owner of these types of commercial properties you also have a lot more rights with how you can handle the tenants, particularly in the case of non payment.

Who Do You Hire?

When you own retail property you will not be using the same type of property management company as you used with apartment buildings. Retails buildings, office buildings, and strip shopping centers are usually managed by national commercial real estate companies. The beauty of owning these types of commercial properties is the fact that the tenants usually pay the property management fee. The property management company will have far less daily work, as the tenants usually take care of all the property's repairs and expenses. There will be some paperwork to complete and maybe a drive-by of the property periodically to ensure the building is properly maintained, but the daily headaches that come with managing apartment buildings just won't be there.

Managing Real Estate Agent Versus A Leasing Real Estate Agent

If the property you are looking to purchase is vacant, you will need the services of a leasing agent. The leasing agent will be responsible for securing and negotiating the lease terms with potential tenants. A managing agent (or company) manages the property once the tenant is in place. The listing agent and the managing agent can be the same person or company. This is often a negotiation point you can use with the leasing agent when discussing commissions. You can offer him the property management contract for taking a reduced leasing commission.

If you will be obtaining conventional commercial real estate financing, the lender will want to know who you have lined up to manage the property, so they can verify the company is capable of doing the job. If you tell the lender that you will personally be managing a strip mall, which is located in a different state from where you live, the lender will look on that negatively. If that is your plan, you better have a different story for the lender.

Security Deposits/Property Management Contract

The same recommendations made regarding the tenant's security deposits and the property management contract in the apartment building section applies to the retail sector as well.

MANAGING REAL ESTATE AGENTS/COMPANIES

Hire Someone Local

I was in contract to purchase a retail building in Anderson, Indiana. The national property management company I was thinking about hiring, did not have a office located in Anderson. Their nearest office was an hour away in Indianapolis. How good of a job could they have done managing a property when they would have to spend an hour of drive time just to get there? I decided I would hire a local commercial real estate company with an office located just a block down the road from the property. The real estate broker had to literally drive past the property everyday on his way to the office. Which company do you think would have been able to manage the property most effectively? Although I never closed on that property, I'm grateful for the education I received during the process.

How Are They Paid?

Property management fees in these types of properties typically run 2-5% of the gross income of the property depending upon the complexity of the property. Some companies charge a minimum monthly fee that may make it difficult for some commercial investors to financially afford their service. However, the majority of the time, you will not personally be paying the property management fee. This expense is usually the responsibility of

> How good of a job could they have done managing a property when they would have to spend an hour of drive time just to get there?

the tenant.

I haven't personally had the best experiences with large commercial real estate companies. It boils down to how good any one agent is within that company. If that real estate agent leaves the company and someone else steps in their place, you don't know how well that person will perform.

THE ADVANTAGES OF HIRING A LARGE COMMERCIAL REAL ESTATE COMPANY

There are some advantages of hiring a large commercial real estate company to manage your property.

You Always Have Someone In Charge Of Your Property

One of those advantages is their size. You will always have someone to take care of your property, even if you don't know who that person will be.

Their Negotiation Power

Another advantage of hiring a large commercial real estate company to manage your commercial property is their negotiating power. Because of their size, they may be able to negotiate favorable deals on your behalf with certain vendors.

It may take some experimenting with different types of property management companies before you find the perfect fit.

LEASING REAL ESTATE AGENTS/COMPANIES

Let's say you are ready to purchase a vacant commercial retail property. You need to find a tenant. Who will market the building for you? This is where a leasing agent comes in. Hiring a leasing agent, in my opinion, is not optional. Do you really want to or have the time to properly market a retail property for lease? It's a highly specialized area, that should be left to a *competent* commercial leasing agent. A commercial lease is complex. The lease agreement contains many different negotiating points that a novice commercial real estate investor will not think of. Once again, I want to emphasize that the skills and the expertise level varies from agent to agent. You must find a leasing agent who is not only knowledgeable, but whose negotiation style matches yours.

How Are They Paid?

Leasing agents are usually paid a commission of 4-6% of the lease value. For instance, if a tenant signs a lease for $50,000/year for a ten year term, then the value of the lease is $500,000.

$50,000/year X 10 years = $500,000   Lease Value

At a 5% commission rate, the leasing agent's commission would be $25,000.

$500,000 X .05 = $25,000   Leasing Agent's Commission

Knowing how to calculate the lease value is important because you will need to have the funds set aside to pay the leasing agent's commission. This is also important to know because the leasing agent's commission is calculated on the initial lease term only, but not on right of renewal options. This can make a big impact on the amount of money you would be responsible to pay.

For instance, using the example above, if the lease term was changed to five years, with one right of renewal for an additional five years, then the lease value would be calculated like this:

$50,000/year X 5 years = $250,000   Lease Value

At a 5% commission rate, the leasing agent's commission would be $12,500.

$250,000 X .05 = $12,500   Leasing Agent's Commission

This commission structure is something I've never understood. The main problem lies in the fact that the property owner carries all of the risk. The revenue from the tenant may abruptly end due to circumstances beyond your control. What if the tenant files bankruptcy? What if the tenant's business shuts down?

A better solution would be for the lease commission to be paid monthly to the leasing agent as the property owner receives the money. However, even this scenario is unrealistic because the commission is usually split between the tenant's leasing agent and the property owner's leasing agent. The leasing agents most likely won't work for the same company during the entire duration of the lease term.

Another problem with the current commission structure is that it doesn't provide the leasing agent with incentives for negotiating powerful landlord protecting clauses.

While I don't like the current leasing commission structure, it is, what it is. Leasing commission rates and payments can and should be negotiated depending upon the situation of the deal.

The Leasing Agent Must Believe In The Property

I know this sounds kind of "out there," but here's why I say this. My first face to face contact with a commercial leasing agent was during the inspection for the property in Anderson, Indiana. Steve (not his real name), the seller's leasing agent, met me at the property before the inspection started. Before I had written an offer to purchase the property, I found that the *lowest* comparative market

> How effectively could Steve negotiate a lease on the owner's behalf, if he didn't believe in the property's worth?

rental rate was $6/Sq Ft. Using that figure, as a worst case scenario, I felt the property could easily be rented and make a ton of money. Steve, however, didn't feel the property was worth leasing even at $6/Sq Ft. "The former Walmart building down the road is a much nicer building. It's only renting for $4.50/Sq Ft." he said.

That may be so, but Steve was not comparing apples to apples. The other property was much larger. As I've mentioned before you will not be able to command as much money per square foot for larger rental space sizes. The Walmart building was also located in an entirely different part of town. This property was located in the heart of the city's main retail area, while the former Walmart building was located in an area that was not nearly as busy.

How effectively could Steve negotiate a lease on the property owner's behalf, if he didn't believe in the property's worth? The property was located literally next door to a property that was commanding $18/Sq Ft. I felt that leasing the property at

$6/Sq Ft, even in it's existing condition, was too low.

Marketing Your Commercial Property For Sale

If your leasing agent does not have your commercial property for lease listed on Loopnet, he should be fired. That about sums it up.

LEASE NEGOTIATIONS

The quality of the tenant and the quality of the lease are the two things that will make the difference between a favorable landlord experience or a poor one. We went over the many different types of clauses you can use to enhance a commercial property's financial potential in the commercial real estate analysis section. These clauses are the same ones you want to negotiate into any new lease agreement.

Evaluate Comparable Lease Rental Rates For Yourself

Don't trust the leasing agent's rental rate value he indicates the property should lease for. As I mentioned in the story just a bit ago, Steve was not comparing comparable properties. You, as the property owner, must decide what the acceptable lease rental rates and terms are. You can always change it later if you find your value was out of line. Just don't make the assumption that because they are the "professional," they know more than you do about the market rental rates.

Which Expenses Is The Tenant Responsible To Pay?

Have the tenant pay for as many expenses as possible. Who pays which property expenses is usually a give and take situation which has to be negotiated on an individual basis.

I would personally accept a lower per square foot rental rate and have the tenant responsible for more of the property's expenses. This is because the property's expenses will always increase and this way, you wouldn't have to absorb the increased costs. The rental rate stays the same and you know ahead of time if that figure works for you or not.

Percentage Rent Clause

Try to have a percentage rent clause added in your lease agreement. The breakpoint on which the clause is triggered is also a fine negotiating point. What's the point of having a percentage rent clause in the lease agreement if the breakpoint is so high that it's unattainable during the course of the lease term?

Insurance

The property owner can dictate what insurance coverage the tenant is required to have. If there is something unusual about the nature of the tenant's business that may make the property more susceptible to the possibility of an insurance claim, then you can ask for whatever insurance coverage you feel will mitigate for the increased risk. Does that mean you will get it? Not necessarily. But you need to be protect yourself and your other tenants as well.

Insurance issues can get more complicated when you are dealing with multiple tenants. One tenant's actions can affect another tenant's business. All of those issues need to be worked out in a manner that is fair for all parties. Also make sure you have a provision in the insurance policy that covers loss of rental income.

241

Chapter Thirteen

What Type Of Business Is Allowed?

Certain types of businesses cause certain types of concerns. For example, if you were to lease a building to a car dealership, you would want to know if they planned on having a service department. If so, that could cause certain environmental issues. You want to know in detail what exact services the tenant's business will offer to their customers. You can dictate what type of services are acceptable on the premise and which types of services are not acceptable. Any change to the services offered by the tenant will have to be authorized by the property owner.

Subleasing

There are times when the existing tenant decides to relocate, shuts their doors, or the company merges with another company. All of these situations may leave you with a vacant property without incoming revenue. If the tenant vacates the property do they have the right to sublease the property? Allowing a tenant to sublease may provide you with income you wouldn't otherwise receive. As a minimum you should require that the new tenant has to have your approval prior to any formal subleasing agreement being signed.

Rachet Clause

During a rental rate evaluation it may be found that the market rental rates have declined. The addition of this clause in the lease agreement ensures that if that happens, the tenant's rental rate will, at a minimum, remain the same. The tenant's rental rate is only allowed to be increased, not decreased.

Rental Rate Increases

Most rental rate increases are negotiated ahead of time and placed into the lease agreement before the lease is signed. However, there is a lot of variation as to how the rental rate increase will be determined. Do you want the rental rate increase to be based upon comparable market rental rates? Do you want it to be tied to the Consumer Price Index? Would you rather have a fixed percentage increase? There's all kinds of way to negotiate the method of increasing a tenant's rental rate.

A fixed rental rate increase provides income security, but with the risk of losing out on additional income if the market rental rates increase significantly. You may decide to combine these options by having the tenant's rental rate increase based upon comparable market rental rates with a guaranteed minimum rental rate increase.

Lease Term

The length of the lease term is an important consideration. Commercial real estate lenders love to finance properties that are occupied with a tenant on a long term lease-it makes them drool. The longer the lease term, the better.

However, there are times when a shorter lease term makes sense, such as when you are redeveloping the property or when you have another tenant who wants to lease the premise at a higher rental rate than the existing tenant pays, but not for another couple of years.

Chapter Thirteen

Right Of Renewal

A *right of renewal* provision allows the tenant to renew the lease agreement under certain preestablished terms and conditions when the initial lease term expires. It is a provision that is favorable for the tenant, although most people, including lenders, think it's a favorable provision for the landlord.

What makes this a favorable provision for the tenant rather than the landlord is for the fact that it binds the landlord to leasing to the tenant with the provisions of the established lease.

First Right Of Refusal

The tenant may want a *first right of refusal* to purchase the property. I can't think of any negative aspect to agreeing to this provision. You have a potential buyer in place when you decide to sell the property down the road. If the tenant does not want to purchase the property at the price you establish, you can then sell it to whomever you choose.

Make sure that the terms of the first right of refusal are specific. The tenant must be restricted on how long they have to decide if they are going to purchase the property or not and how long they have to close on the property. If you don't have the specifics of the first right of refusal included in the lease agreement, the tenant can hold up the sale to another purchaser who can meet your needs.

Negotiating a commercial lease agreement is a process which requires both parties to give and take. Although, that doesn't mean you shouldn't ask for the stars and moon. You just may get it!

WHAT NOBODY TELLS YOU!

1. You must hire a bookkeeper.
2. Hiring a competent property manager is the key to successful commercial real estate ownership.
3. Apartment tenants have way more protection than retail tenants have.
4. Retail lease agreements contain many clauses that need to be negotiated.
5. When negotiating a new lease agreement with a tenant, always ask for the stars and the moon. You just may get it!

CHAPTER 14
INCREASING THE VALUE OF YOUR COMMERCIAL PROPERTY

When you own residential real estate, you can do things to increase it's value, but the value will still be capped by comparable properties in the neighborhood. However, when you own commercial real estate, it's value isn't capped by comps because it's value is derived from it's income. Increasing the value of a commercial property is accomplished by doing one or both of the following:

1. Increase the property's income.
2. Decrease the property's expenses.

Increasing the property's income or decreasing it's expenses can occur numerous ways. Let's go over some ideas that you may want to try after you have purchased your first commercial property.

247

Chapter Fourteen

HOW TO INCREASE THE INCOME OF COMMERCIAL REAL ESTATE

There are so many possibilities for increasing a commercial property's income, that entire books have been written about the various methods available. The key to increasing a commercial property's income lies within your ability to see opportunities that other people miss.

1. INCREASE THE PROPERTY'S OCCUPANCY LEVEL

APARTMENTS

Advertise On The Internet

One of the best ways to increase a property's occupancy level is by advertising the property on the internet, in conjunction with traditional advertising methods. When people are planning to move, they will usually search for housing online. If you don't have your property listed online, you're missing out on a huge pool of possible tenants.

When placing your online ad, do something creative. I once posted a free ad on Craigslist (www.craigslist.org) with the following headline:

DO YOU HATE LANDLORDS FROM HELL?
We do too! We treat you with the respect you deserve.

The headline was unique enough to make someone stop and read it before the other ads. In fact, the property manager received one or two calls a day from the newspaper ad she placed, while the Craigslist ad generated about ten calls a day.

RETAIL

You can easily double the value of a retail property by filling a large vacant space with a tenant. Many savvy investors seek out properties with large vacancy levels, so they can purchase it at a reduced cost. Once the property closes, they increase the occupancy levels, raising the property's value by millions of dollars.

The best example of this was when Donald Trump purchased the American Express building for $1,000,000. The building was occupied with only one tenant, an attorney, who was suing the property owner. Trump knew that with some cosmetic improvements, he would be able to find suitable tenants for the property. With the help of his leasing agent and property management team, the building is now completely occupied. The increase to the occupancy level increased the property's value to $400,000,000. At the time everyone thought Trump was crazy for purchasing the American Express building, but he knew what he was doing.

> **Many savvy investors seek out properties with large vacancy levels, so they can increase the occupancy level, and therefore increase the property's value by millions of dollars.**

Increasing the property's occupancy level is one of the best ways to quickly increase it's value, if are able to cover the property's expenses until the vacant spaces can be leased.

2. INCREASE RENTAL RATES

APARTMENTS

Another strategy you could us to increase the value of a commercial property is by purchasing a property that has below market rental rates. The property would be purchased at a price based upon it's existing NOI. After the purchase is completed, if the tenant's rental rates are substantially below the market rental rate, and the property's occupancy level is high, then go ahead and raise the rental rates. Bear in mind, that owning a fully occupied property occupied by tenants with slightly below market rental rates, is still better than owning a property with a high vacancy level caused by increasing the rental rate too high. Each time a tenant leaves, it costs a lot of money to replace them, so keep the tenant's rental rate at a reasonable level to minimize the likelihood of a tenant moving to a different apartment.

> **If an existing tenant's rental rate is below the market rental rate, even a small increase to their rental rate can yield a significant financial benefit for you.**

RETAIL

With retail properties, the rental rate increases are usually built into the tenant's lease agreement. However, you may find a situation where that is not the case. If an existing tenant's rental rate is below the market rental rate, even a small increase to their rental rate can yield a significant financial benefit for you.

For instance, if a tenant is leasing a 10,000 Sq Ft building for

$1/Sq Ft/month, and you increased their rental rate to $1.10/Sq Ft/month, it would put an extra $1,000/month or $12,000/year, in your pocket. What could you do with an extra $12,000/year? In addition to the benefit of increased cash flow, you would have increased the property's value by $120,000 (assuming a 10% cap rate).

3. ADD COIN OPERATED WASHERS AND DRYERS

A lot of extra income can be generated by adding coin operated washers and dryers at your property. You can either purchase the machines yourself, or you can have a leasing company supply you with everything that is needed. A leasing company will handle all aspects of the equipment maintenance, laundry room cleaning, and money collection for a percentage of the revenue collected. All you have to do is sit back and collect your portion of the revenue generated. Some companies will even completely renovate the laundry room at their expense for a long term contract. Sounds like a good idea to me.

4. ADD VENDING MACHINES

Generating revenue from soda and candy vending machines works along the same line as generating income from coin operated washers and dryers. Most of the time, the companies that place these types of vending machines takes care of everything. You will receive a percentage of the vending sales without any work on your end.

5. SUBDIVIDE EXTRA LAND

Vacant land typically does not generate an on-going monthly income for a real estate investor. However, that's not to say it can't. If you purchase a commercial property that has extra land, you can subdivide it to create a second parcel.

There are a lot of ways to make money off of the newly created parcel of land. Many times, you can market the parcel of land for sell or for lease prior to starting the subdivision process, which helps minimize any financial risk to you. If you find a buyer prior to the subdivision being complete, just make the purchase contract contingent upon it's completion. You can also opt to lease the ground, or construct a building specifically designed for the tenant who will sign a long term lease agreement.

Whether you opt to sell the newly created parcel or lease it depends upon your investment goals. You will still own the original property, that met your investment criteria when it was originally purchased, plus you will have created an extra parcel of land that can provide you with additional income.

In order to subdivide the land you will need to hire a surveyor or a civil engineer. The surveyor or civil engineer will complete all the necessary drawings and maps to submit with the subdivision application. If you create four parcels or less, the subdivision process is fairly easy. Is the subdivision process worth your time? That depends upon the cost of hiring the surveyor and the cost of the subdivision application, along with how much additional revenue can be generated from the new parcel.

6. CHANGE THE ZONING

A property's zoning designation governs what can or cannot be done with the land. TYPICALLY, there is a hierarchy of sorts to the value of land, which depends upon it's zoning classification. Going from the most valuable zoning designation, to the least valuable zoning designation, it is as follows:

Most Valuable   **Least Valuable**

Commercial ➔ Residential ➔ Industrial ➔ Agricultural

Just because you bought a property with a certain zoning classification does not mean it forever has to stay that way. Zoning can be changed. It happens everyday! If you are able to change the property's current zoning designation to a zoning designation that permits the land to have a "higher use," it becomes more attractive to real estate investors, developers, and builders.

You should have already done your homework regarding your property's current zoning classification and

> **Most cities have a "master plan" that shows how the City wants each area zoned by a certain date. If you can help the City bring that zoning designation to the property before that date, it's just about guaranteed your zoning change request will be approved.**

the zoning classification of the surrounding area during your due diligence phase. Most cities have a "master plan" that shows how the City wants each area zoned by a certain date. If you can help the City bring that zoning designation to the property before that date, it's just about guaranteed your zoning change request will be approved.

7. CHANGE THE USE

Is there an old warehouse building that can be converted into residential condominiums? Do you see a mansion that would be great as a bed and breakfast? Changing the use of a property can bring a higher financial value to the property. A change of use sometimes requires rezoning and other times, does not. Find out the current zoning classification of the property to see if the "use" you have in mind for the property, is permitted. If the use is not permitted under it's current zoning designation, then you will have to either change the zoning designation to one where the use is permitted, or apply for a "special use permit." Certain "uses" must go before the local city officials for approval regardless of the property's zoning designation.

8. CHANGE THE DENSITY ALLOWED

Let's say you own an apartment complex that has extra land. The local regulations allow ten dwelling units/acre to be built. If you decide to subdivide the land, simultaneously apply to increase it's allowable density. If you are able to get the allowable density increased to 30 dwelling units/acre, then the land will be worth a lot more money to a builder, as it gives him the ability to make a substantially higher profit.

9. CHANGE OWNERSHIP TYPE

The best example of changing ownership type is a condominium conversion. A condo conversion changes the ownership type of a property from separate ownership to common ownership. This change happens by filing certain paperwork mandated by local and state government officials. Once the property legally changes to condominiums, the value as individual condominiums units far exceeds their value as apartments because you cannot sell off individual apartment units.

10. SELL OWNERSHIP INTERESTS IN THE PROPERTY

Let's say you purchased a beautiful vacation home located in a resort area for $1,000,000. You love the area, but will realistically only use the property four weeks per year. It may be wise to sell off four week ownership interests in the property for $150,000 each. You would keep a four week ownership interest for yourself and still have 12 ownership interests to sell. At a sales price of $150,000 for each ownership interest, you would net a $800,000 profit, while retaining an ownership interest for yourself, which allows you to enjoy the property year after year.

$1,800,000   Income From Selling 12 Ownership Interests
-$1,000,000   Cost To Purchase The Property
= $800,000   Profit

When selling ownership interests, certain state laws must be complied with. It's essential to hire the proper professionals to guide this transaction.

11. ALLOW A BILLBOARD TO BE PLACE ON THE PROPERTY

Most cities do not like to approve new billboard structures. If you find that the city where your commercial property is located doesn't have tight billboard restrictions, allowing a company to place a billboard on your property may be a viable option to generate additional revenue. The property must be in a location where exposure to a large number of people is ensured.

Most of the time the billboard company leases the land. Negotiate a long term lease with a reputable billboard company. You want additional income without any extra work after the initial approval from the city is obtained from the local government officials. You don't want the headache of selling advertisements or maintaining the physical structure itself. The billboard company should also pay the expense of bringing the application before the city for approval and for the cost to build the structure itself.

12. LEASE YOUR WATER RIGHTS

Do you own water rights? If so, what are you doing with them? Leasing your water rights (never sell them) allows you to financially benefit from that asset. Go to my website, www.monicavillasenor.net, to see a newspaper ad placed by a person seeking water rights.

13. SELL YOUR AIR RIGHTS

We've already discussed what air rights are. If you are sure you won't need to increase the height of your property, sell your air rights to a developer who can use them.

14. ACCEPT CREDIT CARDS AND CHARGE A FEE FOR THE PRIVILEGE

Let's face it, we all get into a financial pinch sometimes and have to whip out a credit card to get by. Offer your tenants the ability to pay their rent with a credit card. Almost anyone can be set up to accept major credit cards. The typical fee charged by a credit card issuer is between 1.15% to 3% of the amount charged. Charge the tenant a 5% fee if they choose to pay their rent by credit card. The fee you charge to the tenants would probably be less than their late fee. Then, you keep the difference between the 5% fee you charge the tenant and the fee the credit card issuer charges you.

15. SEND UNCOLLECTED RENT OWED TO COLLECTIONS

Tenants up and bail all of the time leaving you with a large unpaid rent balance. Most of the time, these types of tenants will leave their apartment unit trashed too. Between the unpaid rent and the repairs needed to the fix up the unit, you can easily be owed over $2,000. The former tenant shouldn't get away with that kind of irresponsible behavior. Any uncollected money owed to you from a former tenant should be handed over to a collection agency. I personally feel better knowing that, at a minimum, my former tenant's credit rating will be ruined. Once in a while you will be surprised to find a check in the mail when an outstanding bill has been collected by the collection agency.

Simple measures can create additional revenue streams from a commercial property. It doesn't take much, just a little thought and some action. Purchase the property at a price based upon it's current NOI, with a specific plan in mind to increase the property's income and value. Don't justify paying a higher price than you should for a property because you plan to increase it's income.

DECREASING THE PROPERTY'S EXPENSES

1. LOWER THE PROPERTY TAXES

I've never gone through the process of appealing a property's assessed value, but I've been told it's not difficult to do. You will need to contact the tax assessor's office of the county where the property is located. Ask what is needed to petition for a reduction in the property's assessed value.

> You must provide documentation that supports why you believe the property should be assessed for less than it's currently assessed. You can't just say you "feel" that the current amount of property taxes you pay is too much money and expect to have it lowered.

You must provide documentation that supports why you believe the property should be assessed for less than it's currently assessed. You can't just say you "feel" that the current amount of property taxes you pay is too much money and expect to have it lowered. You might submit the property's Profit/Loss statement. What about the local crime levels? If a crime report indicates increased criminal activity, you may use that report to support a decrease in value. What about the property's rent roll? Do they show a reduction in income from the time you purchased the property? You can also ask for a reduction of the assessed value of the property based upon reclassifying certain elements of the property from real property to personal property (We will discuss this in Chapter 17.).

All of these things can be used to support your request to reduce the assessed value of your property, thereby reducing the property tax amount due. Even if it's a long shot, there's nothing to lose.

2. LOWER UTILITY COSTS

The most common utilities that the landlord pays is water and gas. If you, as the property owner, are paying the utility costs, there's a lot of things you can do to lower those expenses. While the electricity bill is usually paid by the tenant, we will discuss it too.

Electricity

Is the consumption of electricity for each apartment unit or rental space individually metered? If so, have the electric bill sent directly to the tenant. If they are not, check to see what it would take to individually meter those units. If it's just not financially feasible to individually meter each unit, that's okay. At least you have researched your options.

Technology may be helpful now, and in the future, with decreasing electricity expenses. For example, there is a new device that uses electricity during the hours when it's the cheapest price and stores it in a large battery. When electricity is need during peak hours, power is drawn from the battery, thereby lowering your electric bill significantly.

Water

Let's now go onto water. How can you save money on something you have no control over, such as a tenant's water usage? How about switching to water reducing devices, such as low flow toilets or water reducing shower heads? Placing water saving devices can be done each time you ready an apartment for a new tenant.

Another important issue regarding water usage I want you to be aware of, is unpaid tenant water bills. In certain cities, the property owner is ultimately responsible for the water bill, even if the water bill is in the tenant's name. Any unpaid water bill associated with the property may be placed as a lien on the property. There have been incidents where properties were auctioned off, without the property owner even being aware that there was ever a problem, as a result of an unpaid water bill. If the water bill is sent directly to the tenant, sign up for third party notification so you won't be caught paying a water bill that was supposed to be paid by the tenant.

Gas

Is the property's hot water heated by a common broiler? If so, that can cost a pretty penny in heating costs, especially during the winter months. I should know. The condo conversion property is a perfect example of this. It costs over $1,000/month to heat the water that serves the 24 apartment units. If individual instant hot water heaters were installed at a cost of $1,000 each, the total cost would be $24,000. From that point on, the savings would be $1,000/month or $12,000/year. It would take only two to three years to recoup the expense of installing the individual hot water heaters.

Saving $1,000/month would increase the property's NOI, causing the property's value to increase by $120,000 (assuming a 10% cap rate). The increase to the property's value would continue to increase over time as well, because utility costs never go down. While it's true that the savings during the first year would be $12,000, with each year the savings would increase each time the price of gas increases.

For example, let's say in ten years the cost to heat the water for the 24 units would have been $1,600/month. By having individual water heaters, at that point you would be saving $19,200/year. Instead of the property's value increasing by $120,000 like in the first year, after ten years the property value would have increased by $195,000. These are the kind of improvements you want to spend money on. They pay off year, after year, after year.

Even if my intent was to hold onto the condo conversion property long term, instead of converting the apartments to condominiums, installing individual hot water heaters would be a smart financial move because the return on investment is so high. When analyzing potential commercial properties to purchase, remember that this can be done.

There's a difference between being frugal and being cheap. It's great to be frugal, but it's expensive to be cheap.

3. LOWER REPAIR COSTS

There's a difference between being frugal and being cheap. It's great to be frugal, but it's expensive to be cheap. I've seen the poorest quality of repairs done because the former property owner wanted repairs done at the cheapest price. For instance, I've seen stereo wire used in a light switch. Find a trusted person who will do the job the right way, the first time. If you look for the cheapest route, sometimes you will have to pay twice for the repair because it was done by someone who was incompetent and messed it up. You will probably go through quite a few contractors or handymen before you find someone who is trustworthy, does a great job, and is reasonable with their rates.

> **Moving is a pain in the butt. Nobody likes to move. If a tenant is renting an apartment from you, he'll stay until there is something wrong, that is so compelling, it is worse than the hassle of moving.**

4. LOWER TENANT TURN OVER RATES

Are your rental rates too high? Do you not respond quickly to tenant's work order requests? Do you treat your tenants with disrespect? Do you not come through when asked? Do whatever is necessary to keep good tenants. Moving is a pain in the butt. Nobody like to move. If a tenant is renting an apartment from you, he'll stay until there is something wrong, that is so compelling, it is worse than the hassle of moving.

If tenants are leaving, find out why. The only two acceptable answers should be to purchase a home or to move out of town. Only by asking will you find the source of any problems. It simply costs too much money to find a new tenant and fix up a vacant unit. Avoid losing tenants by striving to keep them as happy as possible.

5. REFINANCE THE MORTGAGE TO OBTAIN A LOWER INTEREST RATE

While reducing the interest rate on the property's mortgage

won't change the property's value, it will make a huge difference to your cash flow. A reduction of 1% on the interest rate of a $200,000 residential mortgage may not make a huge difference to the monthly payment. However, on a $2,000,000 mortgage, that 1% interest rate reduction is a savings of $20,000/year. What if you could reduce the interest rate 2%? That reduction would be a savings of $40,000/year. Most people live on that amount of money! If there is an existing mortgage on the property that can be refinanced at a lower interest rate, it will significantly lower the monthly mortgage payments. There's generally a lot of fees associated with refinancing a commercial mortgage, but you must take advantage of low interest rates while you can. It is worth the effort!

Get as many streams of income from each property as possible. You must constantly question how you can increase the value of your commercial property. The more you actively search for ideas, the easier they will come to you. The search for a new commercial property to purchase may also spark ideas for increasing the value of a commercial property you already own.

WHAT NOBODY TELLS YOU

1. Being frugal pays off, being cheap does not.
2. Increasing the income of commercial real estate increases it's value.
3. Increasing the value of commercial real estate may come by decreasing it's expenses.
4. Make improvements to your commercial property that will pay off not only now, but in the future as well.
5. The more streams of revenue your property generates, the

Chapter Fourteen

more money you will make.

CHAPTER 15
LAND DEVELOPMENT

There are so many factors involved in land development, it would be impossible to provide everything one should know about it in just one chapter. I don't want to spend too much time discussing land development, as my experience is limited. However, it seems there just aren't many resources available dedicated to providing the information needed for novice real estate developers embarking on their first developmental project. I will share with you some of the things I learned from doing the condo conversion project regarding the subdivision and developmental process which you may find helpful.

It's not really the fact that there's not enough land available that makes it valuable, rather the high cost of bringing the amenities to the property which we have grown accustomed to, that gives it value.

Chapter Fifteen

THEY'RE NOT MAKING ANY MORE OF IT

We have all heard the saying, "They're not making any more of it." as the reason why land is valuable. The thing is, there's vast amounts of unutilized land on earth. It's easy to see if you travel on an airplane and look out the window. However, most of that land is not valuable. Why? Because, most of the time, people want to live in areas with nice weather, affordable housing, full utility services , and local shopping. It's not really the fact that there's not enough land available that makes it valuable, rather the high cost of bringing the amenities to the property which we have grown accustomed to, that gives it value.

THE BENEFIT OF LAND DEVELOPMENT

There's a lot of money to be made from land development. You can take a parcel of land, slice it into smaller pieces, and then sell each piece at a much higher price than you could when the property was one large piece.

> I liken it to buying in bulk from Costco. You can buy a package of 20 candy bars for the wholesale price of 25¢ per piece, then turn around and sell each individual candy bar for the retail price of 75¢ per piece.

I liken it to buying in bulk from Costco. You can buy a package of 20 candy bars for the wholesale price of 25¢ per piece, then turn around and sell each individual candy bar for the retail price of 75¢ per piece. Purchasers have no problem paying the

266

retail price for a candy bar, because they don't want to purchase an entire box, when they only desire one candy bar. That is how land development works too. Developers can purchase a large parcel of land at a wholesale price, slice it into the smaller sizes most people desire, and in the process make a ton of money.

THE DOWNSIDE OF LAND DEVELOPMENT

It's Difficult To Obtain Financing

A lender will look at your personal finances to qualify the land acquisition loan. This is because land is not considered an investment property. It does not generate income, therefore the lender must be confident in your ability to repay the loan with your personal resources. If you are able to obtain an land acquisition loan, the lender will generally only approve you for up to 50% of the land's "as is" value.

It Takes A Lot Of Money

If there's a ton of money to be made in land development why don't more people do it? Because it's expensive! The high expense factor immediately eliminates a large portion of those people who may be interested in pursuing land development. You will need to have access to enough money to pay the mortgage expense (if you are even able to get one), your personal living expenses, developmental costs, such as bringing utilities to the development, and developmental fees such as subdivision application fees, plan check fees, building permit fees, inspection fees, connection fees, and impact fees. The list of developmental costs goes on and on. The costs are not static either. They consistently change. A contingency amount must be set aside in anticipation of the changes to the costs of the project.

It Takes A Long Time

Land development also takes a LONG time to complete. It can take months, years, or even decades to complete a project. You will be working with government officials who don't have quite the same motivation level you do to get things processed quickly.

The speed of the development's progress also relies on your team members. Your surveyor, engineer, architect, and attorney all work at different speeds. While they all work together simultaneously, you can only go as fast as your slowest team member. If one person on your team doesn't finish their paperwork in a timely fashion, your other team members will not be able to complete their paperwork .

> You will be working with government officials who don't have quite the same motivation level you do to get things processed quickly.

It's Riskier Than Other Commercial Real Estate Activities

With it's high cost and long time frame, land development is much riskier than other types of commercial real estate activities. Many things about the developmental process are out of your control. For instance, you may purchase the land and in the meantime the real estate market could significantly soften, making your project financially impossible. At that point you would have to cover the carrying costs until the real estate market corrects itself, walk away from the project losing all of your money, or if possible, sell the project to another developer.

You also do not know definitively if the local government officials will even approve your project until you have spent quite a bit of money going through the subdivision process. You also have to thread around any issues the neighbors may have about the development because neighborhood opposition can quickly kill a project.

HOW TO CONTROL THE RISK OF LAND DEVELOPMENT

You can control the financial risk that comes with land development. The way most developers lower their financial risk is by tying the property up with either a purchase option or with a purchase contract so they don't have to come up with a large sum of money prior to receiving approval from the government officials.

Purchase Option

You can control your risk in land development by using purchase options. A purchase option enables you to tie the property up, without having to come up with the cash to purchase it. The seller cannot sell the property to anyone else during the option period. A non refundable option deposit is collected from the purchase option buyer. The amount of the option deposit is entirely up to whatever is negotiated between you and the property owner. Large parcels of land can be controlled with a purchase option for as little as $100.

If you fail to purchase the property during the option period, the seller keeps the option deposit. While there is the risk of losing your option deposit, a purchase option is a much safer bet than putting a large sum of cash up-front to purchase the land. If you do exercise your purchase option, the option deposit usually is applied towards the purchase price, depending upon how the purchase option contract was negotiated.

Purchase Contract

You also have the option of controlling a property with a purchase contract. You would enter into a purchase contract with the owner which would be contingent upon obtaining approval from the proper authorities. The clauses for which you would be willing to move forward with the purchase must be very concise.

For instance, you may have been successful in obtaining approval from the government officials, but only with so many conditions, that it would make the project financially impossible. If the purchase contract is contingent solely upon you receiving an approval, then you would still be obligated to move forward with the purchase or be at risk of losing your earnest deposit.

The only benefit I see to going with a purchase contract route over a purchase option, is the ability to have your earnest deposit returned. Since land development takes so long, the property owner may not want to tie up his property without ensuring some kind of financial compensation is guaranteed. A purchase option enables the property owner to financially benefit whether the option holder exercises his option or not. A purchase contract doesn't necessary guarantee the property owner will sell the property or receive any financial payment.

FINDING LAND TO DEVELOP

Establish Your Criteria

Once again, before you go out to find a suitable parcel to develop, you must know what you are looking for. What is needed in the area? What is in high demand, but lacking? Is it retail centers, office buildings, affordable housing, or mixed use developments? Can you bring something new to the area? Each town or city has different needs. Once you figure out which kind of development is needed, YOU can provide the solution.

For example, on a trip to Redding, California to visit my family, I saw a dire lack of affordable home ownership opportunities in the area. The median priced home was around $300,000, but the median household income was only around $35,000. I was literally disgusted by the lack of affordable home ownership opportunities available. How would young families be able to climb the ladder to wealth that comes with home ownership, when they were priced out of the market?

> I was literally disgusted by the lack of affordable home ownership opportunities available. How would young families be able to climb the ladder to wealth that comes with home ownership, when they were priced out of the market?

The simple answer was that they couldn't. They would have

271

to either rent a house or an apartment or move to a city that provided more affordable home ownership opportunities. Neither choice was good. I decided to do something about the situation by seeking out a property that would be suitable for a condominium conversion.

A condominium conversion was a new concept in the area, which can be a double edge sword. On the positive side because it was a new concept, it would receive more exposure in the media, enabling the development to be more successful. On the negative side, new ideas are often dismissed before they have been fully evaluated.

Being the first condo conversion project in the city ended up being a big problem because the city's condo conversion code had never been tested before. The code had never been used and it's kinks (and there were many) had to be addressed. To make the situation even more difficult, I had never done a condo conversion or any other type of development before, so it was like the blind leading the blind. After working on the project a year, we finally received an approval from the city officials.

I made the decision to do the condo conversion project in that particular area because the area lacked affordable home ownership opportunities. Once I knew which type of development I was going to move forward with, I was able to search for a suitable property.

Find Properties That Are Not Listed For Sale

Developers are usually better off finding property that fits their criteria and then contacting the property owners directly. Property ownership information is public record. Many times the information can be obtained over the internet. If not, a telephone call to the county recorder's office may be all that is needed to obtain the information. Other times, you will have to personally go to the county recorder's office or request in writing that the information be sent to you by mail.

Once you have the property owner's mailing address, send him a letter indicating that you may be interested in purchasing his property. If you live close to the property owner, just show up with a purchase contract and check in hand. That happened to my parents. A developer contacted them about purchasing their extra land and my parents decided it was a good deal. After the developer obtained the necessary approval from the government officials, they closed the transaction.

Finding properties that are not listed for sale is one of the best ways to purchase properties at a below market purchase price. A lot of property owner's do not know the true value of their land because it never crossed their mind to sell it. If a real estate agent gets involved, he will want the highest price possible, to earn a higher commission.

DUE DILIGENCE

You will actually be performing a lot of the due diligence before you ever make contact with the property owner. The due diligence with land development is a bit different than it is with property that is already improved. Additional reports will be needed to ensure a development is viable.

1. Soil Samples

A soil sample must be submitted to the proper officials to

ensure that the soil is conducive to the specific development type. For instance, you wouldn't want to build homes on expansive soil, as it would cause the foundation and walls to crack. You also wouldn't want to plan a development with an underground parking garage, only to find out in the middle of the project, that there is bedrock five feet down which would financially ruin the project.

2. Environmental Reports

Is there something that was once on that property that has potentially contaminated it? The need to obtain environmental reports was discussed earlier and you know the dangers of buying land or developed property where there is a possibility of environmental contamination.

3. Wetlands

Is there a unique species that lives on the land that will prevent you from building on certain areas of it or on the entire property? Many protected species are found in wetlands. You don't want to find out about it after you have already purchase the property.

4. Property Access

What kind of easements are there on the property? Is there access to the property or is it "land locked?" Will your proposed development interfere with any existing easements? If so, you will need to propose how that will be accommodated. Easements are found on a preliminary title report, which can be obtained from a local title company.

5. Zoning

The property's zoning and land use needs to be verified. You shouldn't trust the seller's word regarding the property's zoning, as it could have changed without his knowledge. You will also need to know the minimum lot size, setback requirements, utility requirements, building height restrictions, and other similar zoning restrictions before you can properly design your project.

You may also find that the property has no zoning classification. An approval from the local officials would still be needed, but should be a relatively easy process, as there is nothing specifically prohibited.

If you will need apply to have the zoning designation changed to bring your development forward, specify that requirement in the purchase contract.

6. Contact A City Planner

This is an important step. Meet with a city planner to run the project by him. See what his reaction is to your project idea. Is it favorable or unfavorable? He may be able to inform you of possible problems that you hadn't thought of and suggest solutions to those problems. Ask him what he would do with the property if he owned it. He may come up with a better idea for the property than the existing project you had in mind.

7. Research The Subdivision And Building Codes

Subdivision and building codes change all the time. If you have done a subdivision before, the codes may have changed from the last time you developed a property. Or, you may be doing a development in a different city and state than the last time.

Don't rely on someone else's knowledge of the subdivision and building codes, as it may be lacking. With the condo conversion project, I studied the subdivision codes on the local and state level to ensure that when the project was presented to my assigned planner, I could speak with confidence regarding what was or was not required with the development. Even as a novice developer, I was able to educate seasoned professionals on certain requirements they were not aware of. The success or failure of your project is up to you.

8. Run The Project Idea By Your Team Members

When you run your project idea by each individual team member you will be able to get numerous opinions about it's viability. Each team member will look at the proposed project from his unique point of view.

> Even as a novice developer I was able to educate seasoned professionals on certain requirements they were not aware of.

For instance, let's say you decide you want to do a 20 lot residential development. Your architect may tell you to position the homes on each lot to accommodate the beautiful views. An engineer may tell you to position each house a different way to ensure adequate water drainage. Your surveyor may tell you to divide the property in a whole different way which enables you to get an extra lot in the development. Each team member is looking at the exact same parcel of land, but their suggestions come from their unique point of view.

YOUR TEAM MEMBERS

Although each team member has a distinct job, they work together as one cohesive unit. They must coordinate their individual responsibilities to ensure everything is consistent and correct. Some of your possible team members may include:

1. Surveyor

A surveyor puts on paper what is currently on the site. This includes the property's boundary lines, existing buildings, sidewalks, trees, storm drains, etc. This is accomplished by performing a survey. There are different types of surveys. The type of survey you need to have performed will depend upon which type of development you are doing.

The surveyor or engineer will prepare the tentative map from the survey. Many times a *survey* and a *tentative map* are referenced as the same thing. The surveyor will also work with you to see how to best divide the parcel of land into smaller parcels.

2. Architect

An architect will take your conceptual idea for the building structures and work with you to come up with a design. That design is then drawn on paper as a rendering. The renderings are placed on the elevation plan.

3. Engineer

You will need the services of both a structural engineer and a civil engineer. The civil engineer or surveyor will prepare the tentative map. A structural engineer will map out the dimensions of the buildings and compute the structural calculations necessary for any structures to be built on the land.

4. Landscape Architect

The landscape architect is responsible for designing the exterior of the property, which includes choosing the types of plants and materials to be used, taking into account the design of the buildings and the "style" of the proposed development.

ITEMS THAT MAY BE REQUIRED IN YOUR SUBDIVISION APPLICATION

1. Tentative Map (Survey)

The tentative map shows the existing boundary of the property lines along with the proposed boundaries for the new parcels to be created.

2. Site Plan

The site plan incorporates all of your proposed improvement plans along with those items which are existing on the property that will stay. The site plan may include the dimensions of the buildings, utilities, sidewalks, storm drainage, landscaping, parking, signs, lights and other land marks.

3. Elevations

Elevations are drawings that show how the proposed building(s) will look.

4. Environmental Impact Reports

An environmental impact report indicates any environmental impact that may occur as a result of developing the land. You must show that your proposed development will not have a negative environmental impact. If there is going to be a negative environmental impact, you must propose a way in which the impact can be mitigated.

5. Traffic Report

If the proposed development is a retail development the impact of the increase traffic to and from the property will have to be addressed. The findings of the traffic report may cause additional costly developmental requirements such as the installation of an additional traffic light or the expansion of a road.

6. Preliminary Title Report

The city wants to see who the property owner is and what the current easements are. This is accomplished by submitting a copy of a preliminary title report.

7. Other Requested Information

When I submitted the application for the condo conversion

project, I was required to submit the property's current rent roll, plus a list of the tenant's ages and projected income levels. This requirement was specific to my project. You may be asked to submit additional items or information that is specific to your project too, that will enable the city officials to make an educated decision.

The city wants to provide their input into the project. They may also see your development as an opportunity to get improvements done that are on their "wish list."

THE SUBDIVISION PROCESS

You have the property tied up with either a purchase option or purchase contract or you have already acquired the property. You have also performed your due diligence and everything still looks favorable. Now, you are ready to implement your plan. The process of obtaining an approval for your project is called the *entitlement* process or tentative map approval. Here's an overly simplified version of how the subdivision process works.

1. FORMALLY MEET WITH THE CITY

You want to meet with a city planner several times before submitting your formal subdivision application. These meetings will allow you to work out the kinks, that I guarantee you are in your application package. The city wants to provide their input into the project. They may also see your development as an opportunity to get improvements done that are on their "wish list." The city may ask you to incorporate improvements into your project which you are not legally required to provide. That is where the importance of knowing what is or is not required comes in. Despite that fact, the city really has the power. Always keep that in mind.

2. SUBMIT THE APPLICATION

Once all the required changes are complete, it is time to formally submit the subdivision application. Generally, the city provides you a checkoff list so you can be sure you have submitted everything they need to process the application. If you don't provide everything they need, they will send a deficiency notice to you indicating which items are missing.

They may also ask you for items that are not on the list which would allow them to have adequate information to evaluate the project properly. The application will not move forward until the city deems the application to be complete. There will be an subdivision application fee, which is non refundable, even in the event your application is denied.

Waivers/Variances

Most of the time your project will not meet all of the codes. You may be able to design a property that is better looking or provides a stronger financial return if you could get around complying with one code or another. The typical way to accomplish this is by requesting a wavier or a variance. The city has the ability to provide a waiver or variance of almost any code.

A strict definition of a *variance* is a deviation in the developmental standard only when, by special circumstances applicable to the property, including location, shape, size, surroundings, or topography, the strict application of the code denies the property owner privileges enjoyed by other property owners in the vicinity with identical zoning. However, variances are given the majority of the time when requested regardless if the situation satisfies this definition or not.

Vesting Tentative Map

When submitting a subdivision application that requires you to include a tentative map, always submit a *vesting tentative map.* During the application process, laws and ordinances may change that could negatively impact your development. If the new laws come into effect before your application is approved, your project will be expected to comply with the new ordinances. A vesting tentative map protects this from happening to you. You should *always* submit a vesting tentative map.

3. SUPPLY MORE INFORMATION/MAKE CHANGES

Your application will move through the city's various departments where each department official will be able to make comments about your project. They will also have a chance to ask you for yet more information or request corrections. Once the application goes through the system you will gather all of their notes and make the changes necessary and get the information they requested. This can be a long process.

4. APPROVAL OR DENIAL

Which governing body approves or denies the application will depend upon the size of the project and nature of the project. For instance if the subdivision is four lots or less, it can be approved at the administrative level. If it's over four lots then the application may have to go before the planning commission. If your application is approved at that level, then the process may end. Or, if it is denied, the decision may be appealed at the city council level.

If the project needs to be voted upon by either the planning commission or the city council, there will come a point when a date will be set for that to happen. At the meeting you or the city will present the project and answer any questions from the planning commission or the city council. At the end of the meeting you will receive either an approval or a denial.

Many subdivision applications require that the residents surrounding the property must be informed of the planning commission meeting. At the meeting the neighbors have the opportunity to voice their approval or concern with the project. Depending upon the project, the neighbors reactions can range from complete support, to complete community opposition.

> The tentative map approval or entitlement is not granted solely to the developer. It runs with the land. You could choose to sell the project to another developer if you so choose.

5. OBTAIN BUILDING PERMITS

Just because the city has given you a thumbs up on the project from the planning department side doesn't mean you're done.

At this point you can choose to sell the project to a builder to carry out or continue the project yourself. The tentative map approval or entitlement is not granted solely to the developer. The entitlement runs with the land. You could choose to sell the project to another developer if you so choose. The tentative map approval is valid for a certain period of time, usually two to three years.

6. BUILD IT

You will need to have your construction team in place prior to obtaining building permits because once they are issued, time is money. Construction financing isn't cheap. If law allows, you will want to start your marketing strategy during this time as well.

7. SELL OR LEASE THE PROPERTY

This is where your hard work should finally pay off. It doesn't matter if you went through everything you did if the project doesn't get sold or leased quickly. You have probably been in the project for a while and would like to finish it as quickly as possible. You will have either initiated your sales plan or hired someone to do so to make that happen.

10 STEPS TO BECOMING A SUCCESSFUL REAL ESTATE DEVELOPER

Let me break down the ten steps to becoming a successful real estate developer, so you can learn from my mistakes.

1. Have Enough Money

This one I really messed up on. I wasn't prepared for the length of time it would take to complete the development. I could barely scrap enough money together to close the property, yet I still had to find the money to pay the costs of development, in addition to my living expenses. I had to pull in more money investors and that was costly because when you are in dire circumstances you have to offer investors a higher investment return. It was extremely stressful because I'd never been in the position where I had to "rob Peter to pay Paul" before. I have learned my lesson on this one.

2. Buy Right

You really make your money when you purchase the property. As good as you are about calculating the costs of the project, there will be surprise costs. You may have to pay more impact fees or bring the buildings up to ADA compliance.

You will not be able to foresee every expense that will occur. Nor will you be able to control exactly when the project will be completed. You will also not be able to foresee the changes to the real estate market. If you don't have a large enough profit margin between the purchase price and the development costs, which can serve as a financial cushion for the unexpected, you will not be a happy camper. You don't want to put all of your time and money into a project to just break even, or even worse, to have a loss. Buying at the proper purchase price will help hedge against this risk.

3. Start With Smaller Developments To Get Experience

You will make mistakes on every single property you

purchase or development you do. Make the big mistakes on your first few smaller developments. Hopefully, you will learn from those mistakes. Once you have one or two projects under your belt, then move up to larger projects. No two developments are identical, but the process will be. At that point, you will have some experience and the self confidence needed to handle the complexities of larger developments. Remember, we all learn how to crawl before we learn how to walk. However, don't get in a comfort zone and postpone moving up to larger projects either.

4. Work With The City Not Against It

When I decided to do the condo conversion project I was asked the following question by several people; "Have you ever worked with the city before?" When I answered "no," then the general response which followed was, "There's no way the city will allow you to do that." For some reason the City of Redding had a horrible reputation for being difficult to work with. I decided to not form an opinion until I saw for myself if that was true or not. If their reputation proved true, I would hopefully "kill them with kindness."

I never had the experience of finding the planning department difficult to work with. I thought my assigned planner, Kent, went above and beyond his duty and I honestly had a good experience working with him.

Don't go into the city with an attitude. The way you treat these people will have a vast implication on how quickly your project goes through the system, the cost, and if it will even get approved. ***Do not piss these people off!*** You will be spending a lot of time with them and they can be your best friend or kill your project. It's up to you. Life is too short anyway, it's just better to treat people generously.

5. Hire Local, Knowledgeable, People

Every local government works differently. You don't have to have experience working with a certain city, but it is helpful to hire people who do. Try to find a surveyor who knows what the city likes to see on the tentative map. Find an architect who knows which style of buildings the city wants to see built. The city may not know you, as a developer, but when they see familiar names on the paperwork in the subdivision application it will help.

6. Know Both The Local and State Laws

Once again, every city has it's own local statues that may be stricter or more lenient than you are used to. Additionally the state may have laws that must be complied with that are different than other states. For instance, California is known for having the strictest laws and regulations in the country. From a developer's point of view, if you are accustomed to developing real estate in California, you would probably find land development in other states a piece of cake.

If you don't know the local and state ordinances, hire people on your team who have that knowledge. Knowing the ordinances and regulations can be helpful as ammunition if you need it.

For instance, the State of California recently passed SB 1818, which is known as the Density Bonus Act. It mandates that cities must give concessions or density bonuses to developers who allocate a certain percentage of the development towards buyers of low or moderate income. If you, as the developer, know about this law and need a concession or waiver, it may prove helpful.

7. Treat People With Respect

You will be managing a lot of people all at once. Sometimes people act like they are back in high school. Your architect may piss off your contractor and you will have to find a way to get issues resolved. The best way to resolve any issue, is by treating people with respect. Barking out orders may make you feel good at the time, but I can guarantee you that those people on the receiving end won't respect you. I want to foster long term relationships. There are tactful ways to handle almost any situation. I am not advocating that you should be a wuss (Is that a word?). You are in charge. But show people respect and you will receive it in return.

> **Once the facts are there, make a decision already!**

8. Be Efficient

Time is money. If you are a procrastinator you will lose money every day that the development is not completed. You must be able to manage a large number of tasks, orchestrated by many different people. If this is not something that you would be able to handle yourself, it's okay. Just make sure you have the money in your budget to hire a project manager who can attend to the details that need to be handled.

9. Be Honest

Did you promise the city you would provide a certain improvement? You better do it. Did you promise a purchaser an upgrade not found in the standard package at no additional charge? It better be included. While cutting corners may save you money on your current development, don't think you would ever be trusted again. If you don't come through with your promises, it's just bad for business.

If an expectation can't be met, ask the person you promised for a suggestion on how they would like you to remedy it. That way they know you are making your best effort to live by your word. Nothing is more valuable. Nobody wants to work with a liar.

10. Be Decisive

Nothing drives me more nutty than wishy-washy people. Once the facts are there, make a decision already! These kinds of projects are not for the type of people who has trouble making quick decisions. Thousands of decisions will need to be made. How big will the lot sizes be? What color should you paint the buildings? What's a fitting name for the development? What price should you list each property for? I could go on and on. You are the leader. Leaders make decisions.

There are just so many facets to real estate development. However, what I believe is the key element of a development's success lies not so much within the aspects of the development itself, rather in the ability of the developer. It takes a person who can handle mental stress, juggle multiple tasks, while simultaneously making quick decisions.

WHAT NOBODY TELLS YOU

1. Land development can be extremely lucrative.
2. Figure out which type of development an area needs and provide the solution.
3. You must have adequate financial resources to cover your living expenses, in addition to the developmental costs, as you don't know how long the project will take to complete.
4. Buy property for a price that allows you to have a large enough margin for errors, and would allow you to still make a profit.
5. Keep current of recently passed laws which may impact your development.
6. Make decisions quickly.

CHAPTER 16
PROTECTING YOUR ASS, I MEAN ASSETS

I always used to laugh about all of the legal disclosures authors place in their books. However, I must do it too. *I am not an attorney or a CPA*. The advice I give here may not fit your particular situation or be legal in your state. *Always consult with your legal advisors prior to implementing any of this information into your investment strategy.*

Now that we have that out of the way, let's move on.....

We live in an extremely litigatious society. It seems that personal responsibility is gone-it's always someone else's fault. It's pretty sad actually. The fact is, the wealthier you become as a result of investing in commercial real estate, the more in danger you are of being sued. We all know that only those people who have something worth suing, end up being sued.

It is important that you do everything in your power to protect your family's financial future against unjust lawsuits. There are many ways to protect your financial future. One of the best ways to protect yourself is through the use of a corporate entity.

WHAT ARE CORPORATE ENTITIES?

Corporations are legal entities created to limit the liability of it's shareholders. Think of a corporation as a person. Give it a name, like Susan or Matt, if it helps you understand the concept clearer. However, unlike a real person, a corporation cannot do anything without your authorization.

TYPES OF CORPORATE STRUCTURES

There are many different corporate structures in which to hold title to your assets. You can use an LLC, LP, S-Corp, C-Corp, or an LLP, to name a few. The exact corporate structure that best suits your personal needs will have to be determined with the help of your attorney or CPA.

> **Think of a corporation as a person. Give it a name, like Susan or Matt, if it helps you understand the concept clearer. However, unlike a real person, a corporation cannot do anything without your authorization.**

Whichever corporate structure you decide to use, the point is to hold the title to your assets in your corporate structure, instead of holding them in your personal name. You, and any other owners of the property, will become members or shareholders of the corporation. Sometimes you will have to acquire a property in your personal name and then deed the property to your company after the property closes.

BENEFITS OF HOLDING ASSETS IN A CORPORATE STRUCTURE

Let's discuss some of the benefits of holding your assets in a corporate structure.

Your Personal Assets Are Protected From Your Business Financial Obligations

If your business went into a bad financial position, the business creditors would not be able to come after your personal assets or any of your other personal income to collect for the business debts. This is important because many businesses fail. Failing simply means that the business ran out of money.

It's a common occurrence for creditors to be left with unpaid invoices from businesses that have failed. This set up seems unfair to those creditors. However, it's absolutely necessary, as it allows someone to start another business with a fresh start, furthering the country's economic growth.

Your Actions Are Protected

You are protected from your actions performed in the capacity and for the benefit of your company. Let me clarify this further, as I can see how many people may misconstrue what I said here. Let's say your company is sued for a wrongful action you did, while acting on behalf of your company and a judgement for $100,000 is issued against your company.

That judgement is against your company, not against you. With certain exceptions, your personal assets could not be touched. You would have to be named on the lawsuit, independent of your company, to have your personal assets at risk.

In order for an individual to be sued as a secondary defendant, the plaintiff must prove that the corporate veil was pierced.

Most of the time if an attorney is suing your company he will also name you individually as a defendant as well. In order for an individual to be sued as a secondary defendant, the plaintiff must prove that the corporate veil was pierced. If they can't prove that to be true, the case against the individual will usually be dismissed by the judge. However, the judge may allow the individual to be named as a secondary defendant regardless of the facts. That is why it's important to keep all of your personal assets out of your name. We discussed earlier that attorneys decide whether or not to pursue a contingency case based upon the financial worthiness of the proposed defendant. If you don't have any assets in your personal name, it's likely the attorney will not waste his time.

Tax Benefits

We will go through the numerous tax benefits of holding assets in a corporate structure in the next chapter.

The Business Continues After The Death Of It's Shareholders

Just because someone who owns all or part of a company dies, it does not mean the company dies too. The company has a perpetual life span and hence carries on with or without one of it's shareholders.

DON'T ALLOW YOUR CORPORATE VEIL TO BE PIERCED

To maintain all of the benefits of a corporate structure there must be certain things that have to happen and there are certain things that can't happen. There are two major things that can cause your corporate veil to be pierced. They are:

1. Fraud
2. Lack Of A Separate Existence

It is not enough for you to file your corporate paperwork and assume you will receive all the protection that a corporate structure provides. Your actions must reflect that your company is a separate entity.

FRAUD

It should be pretty obvious that a corporate structure doesn't provide protection to somebody who commits a fraudulent act.

LACK OF A SEPARATE EXISTENCE

If you don't treat your corporation as a separate entity, then you are at risk of losing the powerful protection of a corporate structure. Let's discuss how to maintain your corporate veil.

DON'T COMMINGLE YOUR COMPANY'S ASSETS WITH OTHER ASSETS

Commingling business assets with your personal or a different company's assets tells the world that your company is not a separate legal entity. Commingling assets sets yourself up to having those assets exposed to creditors. How do you ensure that you are not commingling assets?

Maintain A Separate Business Bank Account

Do you run your property's rental checks through your personal account? You shouldn't. Even if you had the property in the proper corporate entity, through your actions you are saying, that your company is not separate from you. You will need to have a separate bank account you can deposit checks into and to write checks from.

Don't Pay For Personal Items Out Of Your Business Account

Cut a check to yourself from your business. Deposit it into your personal account and then pay for those personal items out of your personal account.

Don't Allow One Business To Pay For Something Pertaining To A Different Business

Let's say you paid the power bill from one property with a check written off of a different property's bank account. That would not be wise. That's not to say that there's anything stopping one business from lending money to the other business. If you do so, have a paper trail for everything!

Sign Your Title After Your Name

You want to make sure that all of your business correspondence has the name of your business at the top. When you sign your name at the bottom, include your title in the company after your name. For instance, I may sign a letter as follows:

Monica Villasenor, Managing Member
Affordable Housing Investments, LLC

That way, it is clear that I am sending the letter on behalf of the company, not as an individual.

DON'T KEEP EQUITY IN YOUR HOME

This was discussed extensively in Chapter 11.

HOW DOES ALL OF THIS SPECIFICALLY APPLY TO INVESTING IN COMMERCIAL REAL ESTATE?

You want to ensure that each commercial property you purchase is in a separate legal entity. This way if a tenant slips and falls, he will not have the ability to wipe out the equity you have in *all* of your commercial properties, just the one particular property. Does that mean you will have to pay a lot of money for your annual corporate filing fees? Yes and no.

Remember, you are now investing in commercial real estate. One commercial property may have 50 apartment units. That property only requires one corporate structure with one bank account. Compare that to owning 50 individual residential homes and trying to protect each one of them with their own corporation and bank account. It would be a logistical nightmare. If you end up owning 50 commercial properties, I don't think your worries will be keeping the properties protected! I think you would be too busy spending all of the money you're making.

WHAT NOBODY TELLS YOU

1. A proper corporate structure can protect your personal assets from the debts of your business.
2. Don't allow your corporate veil to be pierced.

CHAPTER 17
WHY I LOVE THE IRS!

When I was a dental hygienist, I hated the fact that I paid so much money in income taxes. I thought the system was unjust. Now, that I'm a full time real estate investor, I love the tax system. Whether you love or loathe the current tax system probably depends upon how you make your money.

It's been said that it's not how much money you make that's important, rather how much money you keep. That saying is so true. As far as reducing income taxes is concerned, there isn't a better vehicle to do so than by owning real estate. If you are paying any income taxes, it's because you don't own enough real estate.

You will know you have purchased enough commercial real estate when you are able to say, "I love the IRS!" too.

WHY TAX LAW ARE WRITTEN SO FAVORABLY FOR REAL ESTATE OWNERS

The United States government officials realize that real estate investors provide it's citizens with homes to live in and places to conduct their business, which contributes to the financial success of our country. To ensure that real estate investors continue providing for the country's real estate needs, government officials have created favorable tax laws for people who own investment real estate. If the tax laws were not written as favorably as they are, investors would move their money into other types of investments, causing less real estate to be produced. With supply and demand in force, the price of housing would skyrocket. The government would have to step in to provide housing for the ever growing American population. Government officials are never able to provide services as well as the private sector does. They would make a mess of it and it would cost a lot of money. Instead, government officials opt to give favorable tax deductions, such as depreciation, to encourage investors to continue investing in real estate.

I DON'T SEE THE TAX LAWS CHANGING ANYTIME SOON

The majority of the people who bemoan the current tax system are employees. I should know, I was one of them. I have been on both sides of the tax system. There's been talk about implementing a flat tax system for a long time, but I would be surprised to see it happen. Here's why:

Lobbyists

Let's face the facts-wealthy individuals and corporations hire lobbyists to help pass legislation that's favorable for them. Wealthy folks also personally contribute to the political campaigns of politicians who will vote for legislation that is favorable to their interests. The majority of wealthy people have made their income from either investing in real estate or from starting a business, so they want the tax deductions related to these types of investments to continue. If a congressman supported legislation that was unfavorable for those people who financially helped him get elected, when the next election term comes around, he would not have the financial support he needs. A politician won't risk losing his financial support and so the favorable tax deductions continue.

I'm not saying that favorable tax deductions for real estate investments are a bad thing. I personally think that without these tax incentives, it would be financially devastating to the cost of housing. However, lobbyists and other political campaign contributors are just one of the major factors of why the tax system is what it is today.

It Would Cause Money To Move Out Of The Country

Business owners and real estate investors are smart. They will put their money where the return on their investment is the highest. In the United States of America, one of the best financial returns possible can be achieved with real estate investments. The government wants to keep the economy viable, by ensuring that real estate investors and business owners have incentives to do business in America.

Chapter Seventeen

Most Americans Like Their Tax Deductions And Would Have A Tough Time Giving Them Up

Enough said there.

People Pay Either Way

Government officials are aware of the benefits of having private real estate investors provide the apartment buildings, retail centers, office buildings, and other necessary real estate for it's citizens. If investing in real estate lost it's favorable tax advantages, it would have a significant impact on the price of housing, as there would not be as many homes built because real estate investors would move their money into other types of investments. With the law of supply and demand in play, the inventory of housing, as well as other types of real estate, would rapidly decline, causing the price of existing homes to increase. The American people would then complain about the high cost of housing. The government would try to compensate for the housing shortage by building housing themselves, and we all know how efficient they are (Think about how they paid $300 for a hammer!). It would be an utter and complete disaster.

> Either people are going to pay a higher percentage of their income in taxes or they will have to pay a higher price for housing. It would probably work out to be the same cost either way.

Either people are going to pay a higher percentage of their income in taxes or they will have to pay a higher price for housing. It would probably work out to be the same cost either way. All of these points are reasons why I don't believe that the tax system is likely to change anytime soon.

There are many factors to consider when thinking about the tax system. It's easy for a person who is an employee to say that the current tax system is unfair. As an employee, you have no control over how much money in income taxes you pay. I'm not saying that the current system is perfect. But, what I am saying is that you should learn how the tax system works and use it to your advantage.

Unlike being an employee, where you earn money, pay income taxes, then spend what remains, as a business owner you earn money, then spend, then pay income taxes.

KNOW AS MUCH AS YOU CAN ABOUT TAX LAW

As good as your CPA is, he can't possibly know everything there is to know regarding commercial real estate tax deductions. He may not know such things as, the fact that as a full time real estate investor a loss greater than $25,000 can be rolled forward to offset your future income tax obligations.

YOU MAY NEED TO FIND A NEW CPA

I know I've mentioned this several times before, but I will repeat myself again. As you progress to a new level of wealth from investing in commercial real estate, your CPA may not have the level of knowledge you will need him to have. It may be that you are at a financial level where it would actually cost you money in lost deductions to stay with the CPA you have been using. Your team members will change. This includes your CPA. While you will probably pay more for a CPA who works with wealthy clients, does it really cost you more money? Not if you missed valuable tax deductions by staying with an uneducated CPA.

TAX BENEFITS OF OWNING COMMERCIAL REAL ESTATE

Owning commercial real estate is a business. Unlike being an employee, where you earn money, pay income taxes, then spend what remains, a business owner earns money, spends, then pays income taxes. Commercial real estate ownership is a business. The tax benefits of owning residential real estate is multiplied because the numbers associated with a commercial property are larger.

EXPENSES YOU CAN USE AS A WRITE OFF FOR YOUR COMMERCIAL REAL ESTATE BUSINESS

There are many things, that as an employee, you would not be able to write off as an expense on your tax return, that you can write off as an expense on your business tax return. Some of these expenses may be:

1. Travel Expenses To And From A Property You Already Own
2. Travel And Related Expenses To Look For New Investment Properties

3. Meals
4. Gasoline (Used In The Course Of Business)
5. Utilities
6. Cellular Telephone Expenses
7. Automobile Payments
8. Automobile Insurance
9. Office Supplies And Equipment
10. Warehouse Memberships (Costco, Sams Club)
11. Postage
12. Educational Costs (Seminars, Books, And CD's)
13. Accounting Fees
14. Cleaning Services
15. Magazine Subscriptions

The list can go on and on, but you get the point. Those expenses listed above are items used by most American households. As an employee or non business owner, you pay for these expenses, but do so using after tax dollars. It's like paying 30-50% more for each item.

Those expenses listed above are items used by most American households. As an employee or non business owner, you pay for these expenses, but do so using after tax dollars. It's like paying 30-50% more for each item.

Let's do an example just to highlight this point. Let's say your monthly gasoline expense is $500. You would have to earn $750-$1,000 to net the $500 you would use to pay your gasoline expense, after income taxes are deducted. And you thought gasoline was expensive at $3.00/gallon? You are actually paying up to $6.00/gallon for it!

COMMERCIAL REAL ESTATE EXPENSES

The higher the expenses are for your business, the more tax write offs you will be entitled to take. That does not mean you should spend money unnecessarily because, "It's a tax write off." That's like spending a dollar to save fifty cents. You would still be out fifty cents. Here's some of the larger tax deductible expenses you may incur with commercial real estate ownership:

1. Mortgage Interest
2. Property Taxes
3. Landscaping
4. Bookkeeping Expenses
5. Depreciation
6. Property Management Fees
7. Utility Costs
8. Repairs

DEPRECIATION

Depreciation is the loss in value of an asset or building over time. It is calculated by taking the value of the building (minus it's land value) and dividing it by it's useful life. The useful life will either be 27.5 years for apartments or 39 years for all other types of commercial real estate. For instance, if you purchased an apartment building for $2,000,000, and the land value is $500,000, the depreciation would be calculated as follows:

$2,000,000   Purchase Price
 -$500,000   Land Value
= $1,500,000 Building Value

$1,500,000 Building Value = $54,545 Depreciation Expense
27.5 Years   .

That $54,545 depreciation expense is a "loss" that you would write off as an expense on your tax return, even though you never lost the money. That, in itself, is a huge deduction. But there's more. We haven't even discussed the personal property depreciation you would be able to add to that amount.

Depreciation Schedules Vary

What makes up a building? Is it the structure and everything that is in it? No. The best way to think about what makes up a building is by remembering how most commercial buildings are leased. They are leased as a shell. Sometimes, the building doesn't even come with the HVAC equipment.

> What makes up a building? Is it the structure and everything that is in it? No. The best way to think about what makes up a building is by remembering how most commercial buildings are leased. They are leased as a shell.

I remember this situation being brought up when I was living in my condo. The insurance paid through the association fee covered the structure of the building, but not it's contents. I specifically remember being told by my insurance agent that the cabinets and counter tops were not considered part of the building and so I should increase my insurance policy to cover not only my furniture and clothes, but those additional items as well. I was completely surprised! Depreciation of a building should includes only it's shell.

Many CPA's will not know that the items associated with the building, such as appliances, flooring, blinds, cabinets, and light fixtures should not be grouped in with the building's depreciation schedule, but separately depreciated as personal property. The depreciation rate for personal property is much shorter, adding up to a much larger tax write off. The process of separating the property's components into real property and personal property is called cost segregation.

Cost Segregation

Cost segregation is used as a tax savings tools to increase cash flow by separating out the components of a property into real property and personal property. The depreciation schedule for personal property is accelerated far faster than real property is thereby deferring a greater amount of taxes. Any money freed up by deferring taxes, has greater spending power today, than it does in the future, so deferring the most amount of taxes now is often the wisest financial move to make.

> Any money freed up by deferring taxes, has greater spending power today, than it does in the future, so deferring the most amount of taxes now is often the wisest financial move to make.

Another area where cost segregation could prove valuable is for appealing your property's assessed value. By reclassifying certain components of a property from real property to personal property, it's real property basis is lowered. The cost segregation study can be the "proof" or documentation we discussed earlier that you must submit to support your request to have the property's assessed value decreased. There are companies that specialize in cost segregation analysis and will even prepare the paperwork necessary to appeal the property's assessed value based upon the study's results. For more information regarding cost segregation visit www.costsegregation.net.

REPAIRS VERSUS CAPITAL EXPENDITURES

Replacement of an item is not the same as a repair, nor treated the same way for tax purposes. Repairs are deducted in the same tax year in which they were done. However, a capital expenditure is not. It is depreciated at a different rate. The rate in which it is depreciated depends upon the "useful life" of the item replaced. For instance if you repaired a roof, it would be considered a repair and you would write that expense off in the year the repair was performed. However, if you replaced the roof, it would be considered a capital expenditure and depreciated over the useful life of the roof.

I hope you are able to see the incredible power of commercial real estate investments in increasing your wealth by providing excellent tax write offs not found in other types of investments.

CAPITAL GAINS TAX

There will be a time when you are ready to sell one of your commercial properties. You may decide that you would like to get out of investing in apartments and switch to investing in retail strip centers. Or, the property may have had a high level of appreciation and you want to leverage it into a larger property. Whatever the reason is, when you sell a property and make a profit, you will have to pay capital gains tax unless you choose a tax deferment method.

Pay Now Or Pay Later?

Currently the maximum federal long term capital gains tax rate is 15%. It is scheduled to increase to 20% at the end of 2010. The state you live in may also have a capital gains tax as well.

Sometimes the tax laws are written so favorably that you must make a judgement call whether it is wise to pay capital gains tax now, at the current incredibly low rate or if you should defer the capital gains tax to a later date.

CAPITAL GAINS TAX DEFERMENT METHODS

I have to take a moment here to tell you about something I find so comical. There are quite a few people who sell books or hold real estate investing classes who say they will teach you, "The secret the IRS doesn't want you to know about."

First of all the IRS could care less one way or the other whether you know about this law or not. They wouldn't have made it a law if they didn't want you to take advantage of it. I think those people who say this are playing off of the "Let's find a way to screw the IRS." mentality. Secondly, there is no way not to pay taxes, but you can defer them. That is what we are talking about today. It's certainly no secret.

The reason that I want you to know about tax deferment methods is so you will know how to defer the taxes due. Deferring the taxes due allows you to purchase a larger property, which allows you to build your wealth much faster. Some of the vehicles you may choose to defer taxes with, when you sell an investment property may include:

1. 1031 Exchange
2. Installment Sale
3. Trusts

We'll go over a summary of each one of these options.

1. 1031 EXCHANGE

A 1031 exchange is a specific transaction that occurs that joins together the sale of an investment property with the purchase of another investment property for the purpose of deferring taxes. There are many companies who act as the "qualified intermediary" for a 1031 transaction. Most title companies have their own in-house 1031 exchange divisions that can handle your 1031 exchange transaction.

You can even do a Reverse 1031 exchange where the new property is purchased prior to selling a property. It is a much more complicated transaction and it's cost reflects that fact. It is an option that's available though.

Chapter Seventeen

I've done two 1031 exchanges and the process is very easy. After you find the 1031 company to handle the transaction, they take care of everything else. There are just a couple of key rules you should know about when participating in a 1031 exchange.

You Will Not Be Able To Touch The Money

The profit from the property you sold is sent directly to the 1031 exchange company you have chosen. The 1031 exchange company will hold your money in an account until the replacement property is ready to close. You can opt to take out some of the profit and pay the taxes due on that amount, while deferring the remaining amount, if you so desire.

You Have 45 Days To Identify A Replacement Property

You have 45 days from the date the relinquished property closes to identify a replacement property. You can and should identify more than one replacement property because there are too many things which can cause your primary property choice not to close. If you have no alternative properties identified, you would have missed the 45 day property identification deadline and you would be obligated to pay the taxes due.

You Must Close On Your Replacement Property Within 180 Days

If you fail to close on one of your previously identified replacement properties within 180 days from the closing date of the relinquished property, the taxes on the profit would be due.

I can't stress enough to you how easy this transaction is even though it sounds complicated. The difficult part will be finding a replacement property that meets your criteria within the time frame allowed. You better have a property in mind or in contract to purchase before you have completed the sale of your property.

Watch Out For Insolvent 1031 Exchange Companies

There was a highly respected 1031 exchange company here in Las Vegas that ended up closing it's doors because they had used their client's money for other investments which failed. When their clients would ask for their money to close on their replacement property, it had mysteriously vanished.

Overall, there's little regulation regarding 1031 exchange companies. They usually must post a bond, but the amount of the bond required by law is minimal, such as $50,000, which is almost as bad as not having a bond at all. A $50,000 bond won't help much when millions of dollars are syphoned into failing investments.

For more information regarding 1031 exchange transactions visit www.realtyexchangers.com.

2. INSTALLMENT SALE/SELLER FINANCING

As the seller, you may agree to hold financing for a buyer so you would only be taxed on the gain as it is paid to you, rather than as one lump sum. For instance, let's say you paid $1,000,000 cash for a property and sold it five years later for $2,000,000. The profit would be $1,000,000. However, you may not want to pay the $150,000 ($1,000,000 profit X 15% long term capital gains tax rate) due to the IRS at this time. You agree to a $200,000 down payment from the buyer and you will carry the $1,800,000 balance as a 8%, interest only mortgage. Let's see how this scenario would affect your tax situation.

	Pay Taxes Now	**Installment Sale**
Profit	$1,000,000	$200,000
Federal Taxes	$150,000	$30,000
State Taxes	$90,000	$18,000
Net Profit	$760,000	$152,000

You would have to pay the long term capital gains tax on the $200,000 that you received up front. That would be $30,000, plus any state long term capital gains tax due, let's say, at a rate of 9% or $18,000, for a total of $48,000 paid in taxes. You would be left with $152,000, less your portion of closing costs.

The interest income you would receive monthly from the purchaser would be *new* income. Only the remaining profit of $800,000 would be subject to the 15% long term capital gains tax rate, but the income you receive from the buyer does not include any of the principal balance. Let's see how your yearly income would be taxed.

Gross Yearly Income	$144,000 ($1,800,000 X 8%)
Ordinary Income Tax	$43,200 (30% tax rate assumed)
State Income Tax	$12,960 (9% tax rate assumed)
Net Yearly Income	**$87,840**

The whole point of an installment sale was to prevent paying

314

so much money in taxes. However, I don't think paying $56,160 a year in taxes accomplishes the goal very well.

Additionally you don't know when the borrower will pay off the loan, leaving you with a capital gains tax payment when you don't want it. If the long term capital gains tax rate has increased by that time, you would really be hosed (Yes, that too is a technical word.). So, what's a person to do? Here's what I would personally choose given the situation:

Purchase A NNN Leased Property Occupied By A Long Term, A+, Corporate Guaranteed Tenant

Given this scenario, I would participate in a 1031 exchange, rolling over the entire $2,000,000 to purchase a NNN leased commercial property occupied by a long term, A+, corporate guaranteed tenant. Why? Let me explain...

A. The Profit Potential Is Far Greater Than With An Installment Sale

We have to make a few assumptions regarding the replacement property for this example.

Purchase Price	$10,000,000
Down Payment	$2,000,000 (From 1031 exchange)
Income From Tenant	$700,000 (7% cap rate)
Yearly Mortgage Payment	$560,000 (7% interest rate on $8,000,000 loan)
Net Yearly Income	**$140,000**

How is making $4,000/year less more beneficial than the

315

installment sale scenario you ask? We haven't taken into account the entire picture. Let's go over the facts...

1. You Are Putting More Money To Work For You

You would have performed a 1031 exchange during the purchase of the property, so the $48,000 you would have paid in taxes, would now be working for you.

2. The Depreciation Expense Offsets All Of The Property's Income

The yearly depreciation expense would be around $230,769 (assuming the building is worth $9,000,000, and the land is worth $1,000,000). This paper loss of $230,769 would offset the $140,000 of income from the property. You would actually show a yearly net loss of $90,769 that you could use to offset other income or roll over for future tax obligations. This paper loss would happen year after year, for the next 39 years.

3. Your Income Would Continue To Increase

With regular rental rate increases built into the lease agreement and with any bonus income from a percentage rent clause, there's only one way for your income to go-and that is up! The $140,000 yearly income you receive the first year is the *minimum* income you would receive over the next 39 years.

4. Your Financial Worth Would Continue To Increase

When the property's income increases, so does it's value. This increase to the property's value directly impacts your financial net worth.

5. You Don't Have To Worry About Being Paid Off Unexpectedly

You don't have to worry about being paid off unexpectedly, leaving you with a large tax bill due to Uncle Sam. You also wouldn't have the hassle of finding a suitable place to reinvest your money which would probably be earning a lower rate of return than you were earning before.

So let's continue to take all of these facts into account and see how it turns out.

Gross Yearly Income	$140,000
Ordinary Income Tax	$0
State Income Tax	$0
Net Income	**$140,000**

That's $52,160 more *every year* utilizing this technique over an installment sale! The financial benefit, in itself, is unbelievable without even taking into account all of the other benefits that come with it too. There's no way someone could convince me that this scenario isn't a better option than an installment sale.

3. TRUSTS

Most people consult only with a CPA regarding ways to minimize taxes. Even though your CPA is good at preparing your tax return and number crunching, he may not be the best person to go to for advice regarding tax deferment options. While your CPA will certainly know the most popular tax deferment methods, he may not be aware of other options.

Another professional numerous real estate investors consult with regarding tax deferment options is a real estate attorney. They may also know the traditional tax deferment options, but not much more. I've found the best place to go to find out about alternative tax deferment options is a estate planning attorney.

Day in and day out these types of attorneys talk to people about how to move assets around to minimize tax consequences. They will know of specialized trust that your CPA or your real estate attorney have never heard of. Trusts are also good for asset protection as well because it's not easy to find out who the trust's beneficiaries are. Layered with a corporate structure, a trust can be an extremely viable tax deferment and asset protection vehicle.

WHAT NOBODY TELLS YOU

1. If you are paying income taxes, you don't own enough real estate.
2. Know as much as possible about tax law.
3. You may need to find a new CPA who is accustomed to working with wealthy individuals.
4. Cost Segregation-Use it!
5. Tax deferment options are not limited to 1031 exchanges.

CHAPTER 18
IN CONCLUSION

I started this book by telling you the story of how I was fired from my job as a dental hygienist. Initially, it really hurt my ego. I take pride in my work. In my opinion, the quality of the work you do, reflects the kind of person you are. Knowing my performance was exceptional, how could they fire me?

Losing my job brought me to a point in my life where I had to choose which path I wanted my life to take. Should I use, what I perceived to be a crappy event, to explore alternative opportunities? Or, should I wait out the remaining months of my pregnancy and then return to working as a dental hygienist?

I decided to become a full time commercial real estate investor. My decision was prompted by reading *Rich Dad, Poor Dad*, by Robert Kiyosaki. I realized that if I wanted control of my financial future, the dental hygiene profession was not going to provide it for me. An additional factor in my decision was the loss of my sister, April, eight years ago from a car accident. As painful as that experience was, and continues to be, it gave me an appreciation for life that I would not otherwise have at such a young age. I didn't want to ever look back at that point in my life with regret thinking, "I should have taken the chance."

My situation wasn't unique. Everyday across America people lose their jobs for no good reason. Just a couple of months ago, Cheryl, my bookkeeper, said to me, "You know how you always say there is no job security."

"Yeah," I answered.

"My husband was fired from his job last week." she said.

"Why?" I questioned.

Cheryl always beamed about how good her husband was in his job. He had improved the company's sales and had directly helped lower the

> How do you handle the "blows" that life throws at you? Do you complain about it or do you look for the open door you have been ignoring? Trust me it's there-stop ignoring it!

company's expenses. Despite his favorable performance, he had still lost his job. Cheryl explained how her husband's new regional manager wanted to bring her own people into the company. The only way of accomplishing that was to get rid of some of the existing staff. Cheryl's husband didn't do anything wrong to justify being fired.

"Don't worry," I said. "Your husband will find something even better."

"I know," she said. "He already found a new job which pays $5,400 more per year."

You don't always know why certain things happen to you, but

you can choose how you react to it. Being fired, especially at a time when nobody else would hire me, due to my pregnancy, presented me with opportunities I would otherwise not have had. I've also had the privilege to meet incredible people who I would not have otherwise met. I am so grateful I took the path I did. The last three years have been the ultimate emotional roller coaster ride.

How do you handle the "blows" that life throws at you? Do you complain about it or do you look for the open door you have been ignoring? Trust me it's there-stop ignoring it!

It took a lot of hard work to get to where I am today. I didn't just wake up one day with $5,000,000 worth of real estate, a book, and a TV show. I got myself educated. I took action. I learned the hard way by playing the game and figuring it out as I went. I am extremely luck to have the unwavering support of my husband and family. But what has proven most critical is the consistent belief I have in myself. Failure wasn't an option for me. I never gave up. I found ways to solve problems by thinking outside the box. I just can't express how much the direction of my life has changed since I was fired three years ago!

So, what would I say to the office manager who fired me, if we happened to cross paths? I'd probably give her a big hug and say, "THANK YOU! YOU HAVE NO IDEA WHAT A BLESSING THAT WAS."

I wrote this book hoping to not only give you knowledge about investing in commercial real estate in a fun and easy way, but to inspire you. I hope I fully expressed the consistent obstacles I've had to overcome on my journey to wealth, so you would be inspired to overcome your own obstacles. I wanted you to be able to say, "Hey, if she can do it, so can I." I wanted you to shift your thinking away from, "I don't know how to do it." to, "I don't know how to do it, but I'll figure it out."

I would love to hear from anyone who was helped or inspired in any manner of their life, as a result of this book.

Thanks for reading!!!

PS-Don't forget to watch my reality show, "The Making of a Millionaire." It's been picked up by the ITVI network (www.itvi.com).

PSS-Don't forget to visit my website, www.monicavillasenor.net.

Author Contact Information

Monica Villasenor
c/o Villasenor Productions, LLC
10300 W Charleston Blvd #13-360
Las Vegas, NV 89135
villasenorproductions@yahoo.com

Appendix

WEBSITES REFERENCED IN THIS BOOK

www.monicavillasenor.net
Monica Villasenor's website
www.aboutmonacocondos.com
The Redding condo conversion property website
www.themakingofamillionaire.tv
Monica's reality series, "The Making of a Millionaire"
website
www.loopnet.com
The place to find commercial properties for sale or lease
www.thecreativeinvestor.com
The best website to educate yourself about investing in
commercial real estate
www.bankrate.com
A website where you can keep track of different index rates
www.trustetc.com
A self directed IRA trust company
www.craigslist.org
Do I really need to put what Craigslist is?
www.realtyexchangers.com
A 1031 exchange company.
www.rberona.com
Rey Berona, condo conversion expert website
www.costsegreation.net
A cost segregation company

WHAT YOU CAN FIND AT MY WEBSITE
www.monicavillasenor.net

1. Case Studies
You will find case studies of actual commercial properties for sale that were listed on Loopnet. I show you how to analyze a commercial real estate listing, step by step with these real-life examples.

2. Sample Letter of Interest From A Commercial Real Estate Lender

3. A Sample Commercial Real Estate Note

4. Conclusion To The Story Regarding Property Management In Ohio

4. Updates For Seminars And Other Events

5. Real Estate Investing Educational Products
Sign up for my e-zine for the best information about investing in commercial real estate.

ORDER FORM

THE BEST DAMN COMMERCIAL REAL ESTATE INVESTING BOOK EVER WRITTEN!
By Monica Villasenor

Price $29.95 X _____   Book(s) $_____
Subtotal $_____
7.75% Sales Tax (NV residents only) $_____
Shipping & Handling $4.95 First Book
                             $3.95 Each Additional Book $_____
Rush Delivery   Add $3.50 $_____

Total $ _____

Payment Options:

☐ MasterCard   ☐ Visa ☐ Discover   ☐ Money Order ☐ Check

Name _____
Mailing Address _____
_____
Email _____
Telephone Number _____
Card # _____
Expiration Date _____

Signature _____

Send Completed Form To: **Or Fax To:**

Villasenor Productions, LLC   1-702-405-7646
10300 W Charleston Blvd #13-360
Las Vegas, NV 89135

Visit the author's website at www.monicavillasenor.net

ORDER FORM

THE BEST DAMN COMMERCIAL REAL ESTATE INVESTING BOOK EVER WRITTEN!
By Monica Villasenor

Price $29.95 X _____   Book(s) $_____

Subtotal $_____

7.75% Sales Tax (NV residents only) $_____

Shipping & Handling $4.95 First Book

                               $3.95 Each Additional Book $_____

Rush Delivery   Add $3.50 $_____

Total $ _____

Payment Options:

☐ MasterCard   ☐ Visa ☐ Discover   ☐ Money Order ☐ Check

Name _____

Mailing Address _____

_____

Email _____

Telephone Number _____

Card # _____

Expiration Date _____

Signature _____

Send Completed Form To: **Or Fax To:**

Villasenor Productions, LLC   1-702-405-7646
10300 W Charleston Blvd #13-360
Las Vegas, NV 89135

Visit the author's website at www.monicavillasenor.net

331